THE GIFT OF TODAY

A Memoir and Testimony

by

Dianne Klancir

© Copyright 2007 Dianne Klancir.
All rights reserved. No part of this publication may be reproduced, stored in a retrieval system, or transmitted, in any form or by any means, electronic, mechanical, photocopying, recording, or otherwise, without the written prior permission of the author.

Note for Librarians: a cataloguing record for this book that includes Dewey Decimal Classification and US Library of Congress numbers is available from the Library and Archives of Canada. The complete cataloguing record can be obtained from their online database at: www.collectionscanada.ca/amicus/index-e.html
ISBN 1-4251-0949-7

Printed in Victoria, BC, Canada

Printed on paper with minimum 30% recycled fibre.
Trafford's print shop runs on "green energy" from solar, wind and other environmentally-friendly power sources.

TRAFFORD
PUBLISHING

Offices in Canada, USA, Ireland and UK
This book was published *on-demand* in cooperation with Trafford Publishing. On-demand publishing is a unique process and service of making a book available for retail sale to the public taking advantage of on-demand manufacturing and Internet marketing. On-demand publishing includes promotions, retail sales, manufacturing, order fulfilment, accounting and collecting royalties on behalf of the author.

Book sales for North America and international:
Trafford Publishing, 6E–2333 Government St.,
Victoria, BC V8T 4P4 CANADA
phone 250 383 6864 (toll-free 1 888 232 4444)
fax 250 383 6804; email to orders@trafford.com

Book sales in Europe:
Trafford Publishing (UK) Limited, 9 Park End Street, 2nd Floor
Oxford, UK OX1 1HH UNITED KINGDOM
phone 44 (0)1865 722 113 (local rate 0845 230 9601)
facsimile 44 (0)1865 722 868; info.uk@trafford.com

Order online at:
trafford.com/06-2707

10 9 8 7 6 5 4 3 2

As clay yields to the potter
to be shaped and become a new creation,
we must sometimes give up what is comfortable
and be shaped by God's hand.

~Karen Huftalin~

I dedicate this book to:

My daughter Dina, the light of my life,
who encouraged me and patiently waited
until I believed in myself enough to share
our family's most private moments,
knowing they might benefit
another person...

AND...

My God, who loves me unconditionally and
allows me to start each day
with a fresh slate

ACKNOWLEDGEMENTS

This book would never have become a reality without the love and support of so many dear friends and family members. I would like to thank:

My daughter, Dina Klancir, for making me laugh, for her faith, her patience, her feedback, and for asserting her many gifts from God;

My sister, Bobbie Currier, and my parents, Bob and Mary Ann Sladek, for their selfless caregiving visits and for their assistance in recalling events used in this book;

My friend, Karen Huftalin, who is one of the most courageous women I have ever known and whose quote opens my book;

My friend, Sandra Stengel, for her warm friendship and incredible editing talent;

My friend, Carolyn Mielke, who is the world's best neighbor, friend, cheerleader and proofreader;

My friend, Mary Jane Shoemaker, for her expertise, advice and encouragement in writing and publishing my first book;

My former Pastor, Mike Lawyer, who graciously shared his gift of comfort and compassion with my husband and me;

My friends, Kris & Alan Jones, for being there, day or night, whenever a need arose;

My sisters, Margie Kochsmier and Cathy Bober, for their presence in very trying times;

All our friends and co-workers, but especially, Dave & Eleanor Snapp, Dick & Diane Schmidt, Dale & Carol DeWall, Rob & Karen Urish, Joe & Marilyn McCarthy, Pastor Richard & Judi Bright, Earl Simler, Bob LeFevre, Warren Reckmeyer, Bob Glaser, Donna Mattison, Shirley McPhillips, and Ann Baker for their roles in making our lives just a little sweeter during a most difficult time. You are all angels.

The Northern Illinois Tres Dias Community and my reunion sisters, for helping me to realize that nothing is impossible, and giving me the courage to put pen to paper. I am so grateful to all of you.

PROLOGUE

I have heard that sharing personal stories builds a bridge that Jesus can walk across from your heart to others. I believe that each and every experience in our lives is character building, whether it is joyous or sorrowful. How we handle each experience and what we glean from it prepares us for the next life. Did we learn anything? How did it change us?

I have never taken a creative writing course and I don't profess to be an expert of any kind. I certainly don't have all the answers, but I feel I am a stronger person today for having endured these trials with the Lord carrying the burden. I am a work in progress, but my heart is open and as long as my faith is in God, I will never feel alone. It is my sincere hope that by sharing these personal and humbling experiences, someone else's life will be touched in a way that it might not have been otherwise.

If, after reading this book, you would be inclined to send me your comments, I would be very appreciative. You may e-mail me at dklancir@yahoo.com, with a subject line of *The Gift of Today*.

At the author's discretion, certain names of individuals have either been omitted or changed.

CHAPTER ONE

February 14, 2001

It was a cool, crisp winter Wednesday, but unlike other Midwestern winter days, this was special because it was Valentine's Day.

I awoke with great expectation that my spouse of almost 25 years would present me with a steaming hot cup of coffee before my feet could touch the bedroom floor, give me a very seductive kiss, a long-stemmed red rose, and a cheesy card that spoke volumes about how I still made him feel like the luckiest man alive. In the evening, I would prepare a sumptuous dinner and we would join some close friends for a delectable dessert at a nearby restaurant. Not exactly.

My very attentive husband Larry, who was semi-retired and normally out of bed at 5:30 a.m. because, God forbid, he should miss something, was still sound asleep. No coffee, no card, no rose, and worst of all, no kiss. I watched this handsome specimen of a man slumber away as I gently stroked his face. He had a dark tan from years of working outdoors, receding salt-and-pepper hair, a warm smile and the strongest hands I had ever seen. He had dark brown eyes that penetrated to the center of my being and could weaken my knees. He was a man of few words, but a man of good common sense and worldly wisdom, obtained by and large from the School of Hard Knocks.

Dianne Klancir

For the past couple days, he had been experiencing intermittent laryngitis, but no complaints of a sore throat, no fever, no trouble breathing. He asked if he should go to the doctor, which was unbelievable in and of itself. Being a registered nurse and knowing we were in the height of flu season, I told him to rest his voice, drink plenty of fluids and stay out of the doctor's office where he would probably get sicker. Sounded like good advice at the time.

I had noticed that on the days when he worked his part-time job as a maintenance man for a nearby nursing home he came home hoarser than when he left. So, I encouraged him to take the rest of the week off. But, not my Larry.

Larry was very dedicated to his job. He had retired about four years earlier from the Operating Engineers Union, and found himself looking for meaningful part-time employment as a way to make a few extra dollars and keep himself busy. He began working as a maintenance man at a beautiful, church-affiliated nursing home for about 200 residents. The grounds were virtually manicured and the inside of the facility was immaculate. The floors were so sparkling clean you could see your reflection in them and there was never an odor of any kind detected. There was a certain level of expectation from the administration and residents and therefore, the maintenance men were never bored.

If there was a plugged toilet, a light fixture that needed replacing, or an elevator that wasn't working properly, my Larry was on the job. The full-time maintenance staff were all required to take turns being "on call" in the evenings and weekends, but because Larry was part-time, that was rarely expected of him. However, because we lived so close by, there were several evenings that Larry was called when other maintenance staff was too far away to respond to an urgent page. Without a second thought, Larry would charge out the door to do whatever was needed. I remember asking him once, "Are you wearing your Superman suit or will you change in the telephone booth?" He

THE GIFT OF TODAY

would just laugh. I was proud of how responsive he was to those in need, but I also realized he was not 35 years old, and he needed some rest and relaxation once in awhile. Those words were not in his vocabulary.

I bent over to give Larry a morning kiss and startled him. "What time is it?" he asked in a raspy voice. I told him and said that I would go downstairs and get coffee that morning, thinking it would disturb him that I was doing "the morning thing," but he never flinched. (It took us several years to finally figure out that *he* was the morning person and should take care of the a.m. coffee brewing and dog walking. *I* was the evening person who should close up the house and let the dog out one last time. Once we figured it out and made the compromise, we avoided a lot of arguments.)

"Are you taking my advice and staying home today?" I asked.

"No, there's too much to do over there and they need me. But I'll only work a half-day, okay?" he promised.

"That would be great considering we're going out with Dave and Eleanor tonight and I would like for you to be rested up and feeling better. I love you, you know," I teased, and gave him another kiss. He looked at me rather puzzled. I could tell he had forgotten it was Valentine's Day and that was just not like my Larry. I handed him the romantic, flowery card I had picked out for him and smiled.

As we began our rituals of getting ready for work, he turned to me with this sad expression and apology. "I'm sorry that I forgot about Valentine's Day, Dee. You do know how much I love you, don't you?"

"I don't know anybody else who would put up with me," I said. "But don't let that go to your head. I'm ordering an extra big dessert tonight to make up for being without a card and for having to make morning coffee...." and with that, he pulled me onto the bed and gave me the kiss I had been waiting for.

I smiled. "Don't think that makes up for anything. You're in the doghouse now." I just loved to get that man going. He often joked that my teasing and our quick-witted bantering made him feel so much younger than the 25 years in age that separated us.

Larry drove me to work, as usual, and continued on to the nursing home. "See 'ya tonight, honey," I whispered to him as he dropped me off.

"I love you, Dee. Happy Valentine's Day," he said in his raspy voice.

As the day went on, I forgot the "commercial impact" of the day. It was another hectic day at work and before I knew it, Larry was there to pick me up. He managed to crack a smile, but his voice was worse than when he'd left in the morning. His cough was loosening up, but he seemed to be working so hard at it. I could tell he really didn't feel like going anywhere.

"Do you still feel like going out? We could stay home if you'd rather and just sit by the fire," I offered.

"Oh no, I'd never hear the end of this. We're going out."

I made a candlelit dinner of chicken paprika and dumplings, Larry's absolute favorite, and we toasted each other with a glass of wine. Much to my surprise, there was a card at my place at the table, which he had taken time to choose when he got off work. He apologized that the selection of cards wasn't very good, but the fact is, he could have just let it go. He didn't do that. He made every attempt to find the perfect card from those that remained on the card rack. I loved him for that.

After dinner, he seemed rather tired, but still insisted he wanted to go out. We joined our friends, Dave and Eleanor, in a nearby town for dessert. Once Larry was in Dave's presence, he always felt better. He and Dave complemented each other's personalities. Dave was the

THE GIFT OF TODAY

talker, joke-teller, the more outgoing of the pair. He was a tall, burly guy with thick silver hair and a laugh that was contagious. Larry always looked slight in stature next to Dave, but was just barely less than six feet tall. Larry was a good listener and always laughed at Dave's jokes, but was definitely the quieter of the pair. Yet when they were together, there was mischief in both their eyes. I noticed that night Larry was quieter than usual.

The restaurant was a family-type establishment with a wonderfully huge curved glass pastry case by the front door that was filled with the most decadent desserts I had ever seen. They were all prepared in Chicago bakeries and delivered fresh to this restaurant. It was hard to make a choice. Eleanor and I each picked a creamy cheesecake topped with huge fresh strawberries. Dave picked a 4-layer carrot cake. Larry chose apple crumb pie ala mode. Each dessert was mouth-watering, and each of us finished our entire dessert, except Larry. He struggled more and more to talk as the evening went on and looked so tired. We ended the evening earlier than normal, but we had a good time and I had to get up early for work the next day anyway.

On the way home, there were more quiet moments than not, and when I began singing a song on the radio that we both knew well, Larry didn't join in. I reached over to feel his head, and his temperature was normal.

When we got home, I told him I wanted to listen to his lungs. Larry always loved when I tested my nursing skills on him. When I first began nurse's training in 1990, he would ask me each evening what I had learned that day. I'd explain that we learned to make a hospital bed with a patient in it, and he'd want me to demonstrate the procedure pretending he was the patient. The next time I would tell him we learned to give the patient a bed bath. Naturally, he wanted me to practice that on him frequently. "You can never be too good at that," he would tease. Often times that bath led to more than just the routine nurse-patient relationship. Then I would tell him we learned to take blood pressures, and he'd want his checked. He was even my guinea pig when we had to start IV lines and it was a procedure I learned easily, as Larry had the best veins I'd ever seen. It went on this way for quite some time, until the day I came home and told him we learned how to catheterize a patient, and his volunteerism stopped cold.

As I placed the stethoscope against Larry's chest, he reached up and spoke into it as he often did. "Testing, testing," he would say into my ears. I just laughed and rolled my eyes. Nothing seemed terribly abnormal. He just couldn't talk.

As he brushed his teeth to prepare for bed, he seemed to struggle to get out several loud coughs and then I heard an "Uh oh." That caused me to pause dead in my tracks. He had coughed up about a half-teaspoon of bright red blood. I was really concerned that he had pneumonia, but some of the other signs weren't apparent, so I gave him cough syrup to help loosen any chest congestion. I couldn't believe what I was seeing.

"I would like you to stay home tomorrow and Friday," I scolded. "You need your rest. Will you promise me you will do this and not give me an argument?"

"Okay, okay," he replied, which to me, came all too easily. I was shocked.

Larry gave me a goodnight kiss, and the next thing I knew, we were passionately making love. I never expected him to have the energy for that. He never ceased to amaze me or satisfy me. I was so happy that we had that night. It was the last time for a very long time.

CHAPTER TWO

Getting the Diagnosis

The next two days Larry seemed, at times, to be doing better. He stayed home from work and relaxed in front of the TV and fireplace. He didn't seem to mind, and caught up on some sleep. When I arrived home after work we had home-cooked hot suppers that he would just "oooh" and "aaah" over because he said they warmed him from the inside out. By the time he retired for the night, he had usually deteriorated again as we would spend the evening talking. Then he would crash into bed and sleep away the night.

On Saturday, February 17th, I arose early to attend a Christian women's breakfast. Larry was still asleep when I left at 7:00 a.m., quite uncharacteristic of him, so I just gave him a kiss on the forehead. I whispered that he should stay in bed and rest and I would be home by 9:30. He smiled and shook his head without opening his eyes.

To my surprise when I returned at 9:30, Larry was still in bed asleep. I couldn't believe my eyes. I ran over to the bed to make certain he was alright and shook him yelling, "Larry, wake up!" The poor man was so startled; he jumped up, looking mystified.

"What are you doing?" he asked. I breathed a sigh of relief that he was alright and felt myself swallow hard. I asked if he knew what time it was and he reached over to look at his digital alarm clock. "Wow," he uttered lethargically. "I don't think I've ever been in bed this late in my life." And with that he rolled over and pulled the covers up higher.

I felt his head and he was burning up. I ran for the thermometer, and it read 101.5 degrees. In 25 years, my husband had never had a fever. He was always the picture of health.

I sat him up in bed and gave him a cool glass of water and some acetaminophen. I pulled back the blankets and asked how he was feeling. His voice was still raspy as he stated, "I'm just tired." I knew something was desperately wrong. By this time on Saturday mornings my husband had already put in half a day.

I encouraged him to get up and told him I would make breakfast. I listened to his lungs again and this time the sounds were more diminished. There was also some wheezing that wasn't there before. He got up and began walking around, coughing frantically. All at once, he gave a very forceful cough and a look of panic and fear came over his face as he raced past me to the bathroom. When he got to the sink, he released what was in his mouth—a large amount of bright red blood. I stared in total disbelief and reached for the telephone to call the doctor.

We lived in a small, rural town about two hours due west of Chicago, Illinois. Our physician's office was in an equally small neighboring town of about two thousand people. The doctor was only there half-days on Saturdays. As I reported the situation to the office nurse, she said we'd be better off going to an immediate care facility as their waiting room was full of flu patients and the doctor was already overwhelmed.

That would not be a quick or easy trip. The nearest immediate care facility was in Rockford, about 40 miles away, and it would likely be packed with people. I contacted my insurance company to get the "stamp of approval" on which facility would be covered by my insurance and we were off.

THE GIFT OF TODAY

I had only frequented immediate care facilities twice before in my life and the experiences were unfavorably memorable. But as we walked into this clinic, a very strange feeling came over me. There were no screaming children, no frantic moms trying to keep sick kids from rubbing their runny noses all over themselves and everyone else in the waiting room, and no people arguing with the receptionist about why they were waiting so long for care. In fact, there was NOBODY in the waiting room.

My first thought was, *how good could this place be that nobody is here using this facility? Maybe we should just go to an emergency room.* Fortunately, we were greeted by a very friendly receptionist who seemed almost happy to see us. We filled out the necessary forms and in less than ten minutes we were in a room waiting for the doctor.

The nurse came in to get vital signs and find out why we were there. When I explained to her what Larry's symptoms were, I told her that most likely my husband had developed a mild case of pneumonia and we would need an antibiotic. *After all, I was a nurse and thought I had this all figured out.*

I don't know why I said that because, as an office nurse, I always disliked when people would self-diagnose. Maybe I thought I was making her job easier. Maybe I wanted her to be impressed that I knew what the diagnosis would be. Wrong! I knew nothing. She just smiled and exited the room.

The doctor was a very kind, compassionate, unrushed type. He said that he worked at a different facility throughout the week, taught at the local medical school and worked the immediate care clinic occasionally on weekends. *Sounded pretty dedicated.* He looked at the nurse's notes jotted in the chart and then at my husband.

"Is his color always like this?" he asked me.

"Like what?" I inquired looking at Larry with new eyes.

"Well, he looks almost... gray."

Dianne Klancir

You know, it's amazing, but when you see someone every day you don't always notice those things. Larry's skin was always dark, partly because of his nationality, and partly because he worked outside in construction for years. He had an incredible tan all year round, but it wasn't until the doctor stood next to him and I compared the two of them side by side that I realized the difference. Larry's skin tone that day was gray. I felt terrible that a perfect stranger picked up on that.

Then he asked Larry to loosen his shirt so that he could listen to his lungs. He heard the same thing I had. He felt there were diminished sounds and he heard some faint wheezes, but nothing terrible. He did the usual things doctors do when you go in for an exam, and acted like he didn't have another thing to do all day but focus on Larry. He was so systematic and so diligent with his exam.

Finally, he percussed (sharply tapped) my husband's back, which was something I had never been proficient at. As he was doing this, my eyes widened. Each time he would go over a certain area of my husband's lungs, we could hear a dull thud. The doctor looked at me as if to say, *did you hear that?*

After collecting some history from Larry, including the fact that he was a two-and-a-half pack a day smoker for over 35 years and had quit in 1989, the doctor turned to me.

"You're a nurse, aren't you? I think I've seen you somewhere before."

We decided that it must have been several years back when I worked at a nearby clinic that was affiliated with the medical school where he taught.

He then stood facing my husband and asked him to take a deep breath. When Larry inhaled and exhaled, the doctor pointed out that Larry's bronchus and sternum seemed to deviate to one side. He talked very openly with us and his recommendation was a chest x-ray. However, before he left the room, he really put himself on the line. He told us that my husband had a tumor in his lung, that it was advanced, and inoperable.

THE GIFT OF TODAY

In total unison and with a look of horror on our faces, Larry and I both yelled, "WHAT????"

"I would bet my life on it, but the x-ray will tell all," he stated with sadness in his voice.

As he closed the door behind him and we waited for the x-ray technician to arrive, my husband and I looked at each other like deer in headlights. *Did we really just hear that doctor say that my husband had a tumor? How could he say something like that and then leave the room? How could he make a statement like that without even having an x-ray? Who does he think he is...God???*

We were both in total shock. Larry couldn't speak and couldn't think. He was just frozen. I took him by the shoulders and said, "If you want to get out of here, let's go somewhere else. Maybe this guy is just looking for something to do to pass the time here today. Maybe that's why nobody else was in the waiting room. Maybe the guy is a quack. Let's just go. Come on, I'll help you get dressed and we'll just ask him for an antibiotic prescription and go home. If he won't give it to us, we'll go somewhere else until we get one."

I was rambling as fast as words could spill out of my mouth and the adrenalin was pumping high-octane. Larry whispered, "Sit down. We are not leaving. I want to have this x-ray and then hear what this guy has to say." I sat down. I DIDN'T want to hear what he had to say.

The x-ray tech came in and assisted Larry to the other room. While he was gone, thoughts began entering my head that I should have sent him to the doctor four days ago when he first started coughing and spitting up blood. *Why didn't I send him then?*

I began to pace and cry and I didn't want to do that. My hands were shaking and my lips trembling. I didn't want Larry to see me like that. I just wanted him to be alright and for our lives to go back to the way they were.

I used to tell Larry I felt as though we were living in a Disney movie. We had a beautiful home, a terrific daughter, a peaceful community, a large lot surrounded by mature pine trees where rabbits, squirrels and sometimes even small deer ran through our yard. We had meaningful employment and a great circle of friends. I know that probably sounds corny, but what else could a person hope for? We never expected this.

I dried my eyes before Larry came back into the room. He walked in like someone who had been heavily sedated and climbed back onto the table.

"What are we going to do if this is true, Dee?" he asked.

"It can't be true, Larry. But if it is, we will deal with it.

The whole thing just doesn't make sense," I reassured him.

Larry and I were in each other's arms hugging when the doctor walked in. He beckoned me to the reception area. I was rather puzzled, but I gave Larry a kiss and exited the room.

The doctor was looking at the floor when I came out. He put his arm around me and walked me over to the x-ray light. There in front of me was Larry's x-ray, and although I am not proficient at reading x-rays, it didn't take a genius to figure this one out.

I gasped and cupped my hand over my mouth to keep in the scream that was penetrating my very being. My knees buckled. I went pale and headed for the floor. The doctor and staff helped me back up. He was right. The white mass that almost filled his left lung was huge. I felt totally defenseless – almost like I had been hit from behind with a sledgehammer. My hands began to shake wildly and the tears were flowing. The doctor just held me. "I'm so sorry. This has to be very hard for you; not at all what you were expecting today."

"How can this be?" I kept repeating. "This can't be happening."

The doctor handed me some kleenex and said, "We've got to get it together and go in there and tell him. This isn't going to be easy. Would you rather stay here and let me talk with him alone?" he compassionately inquired.

I had made hospital rounds with physicians and had to share bad news with families before, but this was different—this was MY family

THE GIFT OF TODAY

member getting the bad news—MY husband. Nothing is the same when it's your own family member.

There was no way I was going to be out in the reception area crying when my husband received this news. We were one, and we were going to deal with this together. We would rid his body of this horrible mass as soon as possible and get on with our lives.

The doctor and I walked into the room where Larry was sitting with his head down. He raised his head slowly and looked at each of our faces.

"It's true, isn't it?" he asked, reading our expressions.

I stood next to Larry with my arm around him and the doctor addressed us both. He looked like he would have rather been anywhere else but there at the moment. He didn't want to be right about his diagnosis. He explained the location of the tumor, the size, and the seriousness. He told us it was about the size of a large grapefruit and was wrapped around Larry's pulmonary artery and aorta. The condition was advanced and the tumor was inoperable. That was the part that really hit home for me. *Advanced and inoperable.* Then for the first time, he said the "C" word.

"He has a very advanced stage lung CANCER and will need to see a pulmonologist and an oncologist. There is no immediate danger because he is not in respiratory distress, so I am not sending you to the emergency room. I hear it's crazy over there with influenza patients. He doesn't need that type of exposure right now. I am going to ask you to go home and rest this weekend. I want you to see the pulmonologist on Monday. I'll have her meet you in the ER and she'll review your x-rays and tests and refer you to an oncologist. In the meantime, here's a prescription for an antibiotic to begin taking immediately. I want you both to know I would rather have been wrong today," he said sadly. "Do you have any other questions I can answer for you at this time?"

Is he kidding? I thought to myself. *I could go on forever with questions.* Larry was in too much of a state of shock to ask anything.

He showed no emotion at all. I pounded the doctor with questions about the type, the cure, the prognosis, and getting a second opinion. He was very non-committal about the type, but he said the prognosis was not good and we should begin talking about power of attorney for health care, living wills, and making sure his will was in order. As a nurse, I already knew about the importance of those forms.

I wanted somebody to slap me and wake me from this horrible nightmare I was having, but that didn't happen. It was all real. There was no waking up.

"I'm very sorry I had to give you this information today. I'm just glad it was quiet in here and we had the time to really look at what was going on with you. Good luck Larry," the doctor said apologetically, and extended his hand to shake Larry's.

Larry went out to use the restroom and I looked at the doctor and started to cry.

"What kind of nurse am I that I didn't even realize my husband had a huge tumor in his lung? How could I have been so negligent?" I sobbed. The doctor called me back into the room and closed the door.

"Don't do this to yourself. Very often when lung cancer is diagnosed, it's in advanced stages and no one realized the patient had a tumor. My gut is telling me this is a slow growing cancer. Let me tell you this. I have a son who is deaf, and I didn't realize it for several months. I'm a physician and I didn't know my own son was deaf. Does that make me a bad doctor? Of course not. Sometimes we are so close to situations and people that we don't see when things are going wrong. Bringing your husband in here four days ago would have made no difference in his condition. You're to be commended for bringing him in today when the symptoms made themselves visible. You couldn't have done any more."

I will never forget this doctor and the wonderful care he gave us that day. I thanked him again and dried my eyes. I met Larry in the reception area where we tried to pay our bill, but were waved on.

THE GIFT OF TODAY

All at once it seemed rather noisy, and as we looked up the waiting room was full of people-- mostly sick children, who were crying, fearful and cranky. The staff at the clinic was rushing around and the place was absolutely buzzing.

Larry and I walked to the parking lot holding onto each other as if conjoined. When we got into the car, we stared at each other in total disbelief and I began to cry. "I'm so sorry, Larry, that this has happened to you. We will beat this thing. We will do it together." Larry looked straight ahead, nodded his head positively and squeezed my hand.

We had witnessed one of many miracles that were to come our way in the near future. That doctor had spent over two hours with Larry and me because no one else was there. As soon as the doctor ran the tests he needed and we knew Larry's diagnosis, the waiting room was full of people again. It was an incredible experience and I believe we were sent to that location at that time so that Larry would get the care he needed. We truly admired that doctor who, after all his years in practice, still showed compassion, professionalism and yet empathy. I was so grateful for the care we both received.

CHAPTER THREE

The Weekend

The ride home from that appointment was the longest, quietest ride I had ever taken.

Larry insisted on driving, I believe because it gave him something else to concentrate on. I tried to think of something to say that would be uplifting, inspirational, or motivating. ANYTHING. Words just weren't coming. Larry and I were in shock, and there were no words that flowed in that situation. Hundreds of thoughts—good and bad—came into my head, but no words. *How do we even begin to discuss this? What do we do over the weekend that won't overtax him and yet take his mind off what he was just told? Do we share this with our friends or keep it to ourselves? What does our future hold for us? How will we manage this?* I was a wreck.

There was only one answer. All of this had to be given to God in prayer and we had to trust in that. I began praying in the car,

"Dear God, in all your wisdom and mercy, only You can help us through this. I'm not asking You for a miracle here, I'm only asking that You give us the strength to deal with whatever is in our future. I'm asking that my husband not suffer great pain and that he is able to tolerate whatever procedures are necessary to rid his body of this tumor. My husband is a strong man and a good man. He has

THE GIFT OF TODAY

always loved You. Please do not abandon him. You always say that we only have to knock at the door and ask. Lord, I am knocking...I am banging... please give us strength to endure. I ask these things in Your Son Jesus' holy name."

Prayers continued to flow and I felt a sense of peace come over me. Whatever was to come, I knew that God would be there supporting us. We would never feel alone.

As soon as we walked in the house I threw my arms around Larry. "I love you and I feel so bad that I didn't take you to the doctor earlier this week," I sobbed, still feeling guilt-ridden.

"Do you really believe it would have made any difference, Dee?" he asked. "This is from smoking non-stop for over 35 years. Even though I quit 12 years ago, the damage was apparently already done. Seeing the doctor four days ago wouldn't have made any difference. Without the symptoms that showed up today, the doctor probably would have given me some pills and sent me home. Maybe I wouldn't have found out the truth for a longer time by going in earlier for care. This is not your fault and I don't ever want you to blame yourself, do you hear me?" he said sternly.

Larry and I discussed who we were going to share this with. We knew he would spend time in the hospital, so our daughter Dina, who was living in Madison, Wisconsin, needed to be told rather soon.

From experience, we knew that news of this type traveled rapidly in a small community like ours. We were afraid that one of her friends might find out and call to console her. We didn't want her to find out from someone else, so our first step was to call our daughter. This would not be a pleasant task.

Larry and I each got on a telephone and made the call. When she answered, the only thing I wanted to do was scream, but we managed to make some conversation and ease into this. We apologized first for having to tell her over the phone, but knew that it was our only option.

That poor girl was devastated. She cried and sobbed and kept saying, "No, it can't be! Oh no." She insisted on coming home. We tried to explain that there was nothing that could be done right now and that we might need her later on, but she needed to see her dad. Truthfully, I was relieved she was coming home.

Dina had been a delightful girl to raise. She was a beautiful child, inside and out, and she always seemed happy. Although she was an only child, she made friends easily and shared her things willingly. She was an intelligent child, reading by age three. Not just memorizing a favorite storybook, but actually reading. She performed in dance and tumbling recitals from the time she was three years old, and exercised her musical talent at age eight when she began taking acoustic guitar lessons. She was active in every sport—track and field, volleyball, softball and basketball. She earned academic awards throughout school and received college scholarships her senior year of high school. Larry and I couldn't have been prouder parents.

As Dina turned 18 and began spreading her wings, she seemed to resent any advice or input from Larry and me. While we realized it was all a part of growing up and declaring her independence, it felt at times that the rebelliousness was excessive.

At this particular time in 2001, Dina was 22 years old and living with her boyfriend Matt, of which we did not approve. But we did our best to welcome this young man into our home.

Dina arrived about 11:00 p.m. that night, with Matt. He had insisted on driving her to see her dad and he also wanted to see Larry. Until Dina arrived, Larry didn't feel much like eating, he talked very little, and just sat in front of the fireplace watching TV. When Dina walked in the door, she came in with a smile and a positive attitude that was just what her dad needed. I can't imagine how hard that was for her. In her hand was a basket full of all her dad's favorite goodies. There

THE GIFT OF TODAY

were Snicker® bars, potato chips and Pepsi®. She knew what would put a smile on her dad's face. It did my heart good to see him smile for the first time all day, even if it meant he would be eating all that junk. Dina had a very positive effect on Larry.

Larry was 50 years old when Dina was born. He adored her from the first moment he laid eyes on her. Their relationship was almost more like that of a grandfather and granddaughter because of their age difference and because she could get away with anything if she smiled at him. He just never wanted her to be angry with him.

Dina gave him a big hug and I could see her fighting back the tears. I didn't think he was going to let go of her. "Thanks for coming home, punkie." He had called her that since she was an infant and that name has stuck with her to this day. "I'm so glad you're here." he said simply. Dina wouldn't have been anywhere else. She was her father's daughter.

I remembered the day she was born and he held her for the first time. Larry had large hands and they just embraced her little body that was wrapped so tightly in a hospital blanket. He stared at her and his eyes welled up with tears. He couldn't believe how beautiful she was. We talked about what we envisioned for her future—she would be a terrific athlete, have a great sense of humor, she would play piano with the long fingers she had, and Larry knew she would knock the guys dead. We even discussed the boy she would marry some day and the place we would have her wedding reception. Sounds ridiculous, I know, but she was everything we had ever dreamed of.

A couple weeks after we brought her home from the hospital, she developed colic. I walked the floors with her all day while she cried and screamed. After several hours, I felt like joining her, and no matter what I did, that seemed to be the pattern. Larry would come home from work and take her from me so that I could prepare supper. He would lay down on our bed and place her on his chest. She'd let out a big sigh and immediately fall fast asleep. It was almost like she was saying, *'Thank goodness you're home.'* He had a special way with her from day one. She felt very secure with him.

I cannot remember how late we stayed up that evening, but I do remember that we needed to take a family picture that weekend. My sister, Cathy, was putting together a gift for my parents' 50th wedding anniversary and needed a picture from each family that would fit into a 4" x 6" vertical slot. Every family picture I had of the three of us was horizontal, rather than vertical. So, with Dina's boyfriend there to take a photo, we decided to do this. The picture was to be silk-screened onto a quilted wall hanging for my parents with their wedding picture in the middle and their four daughters' families each featured in a corner. It was a great idea, but it wasn't the picture of our family that I would have wanted hanging on my parents' wall forever. Every time I see that photo, I am reminded of the state of shock Larry was in that weekend, and how the three of us fought to smile for that picture.

I recall that we played board games, talked and made attempts at light humor, and that I didn't get much sleep that night. I also remember briefly calling my minister and leaving a message that Larry had been diagnosed with lung cancer, and asking that his name be put on the prayer chain immediately.

The following morning I slipped out to go to church while everyone was still sleeping. I must have looked awful when I arrived, and one of our dear friends met me at the door. He took one look and asked, "Dianne, are you okay?" I remember saying in an almost trance-like state, "Larry has lung cancer, and it's inoperable. This is very serious." His horrific expression told me he understood the magnitude of what I was saying. He gave me a hug and told me he and his wife would talk with me after the service.

With a tremble in his voice, Pastor Mike made an announcement

THE GIFT OF TODAY

to the congregation before the service began, telling of Larry's news. The congregation gasped. I wanted to be so brave that day, but my tears started flowing with the first hymn as I sat in the pew alone. I remember that there was an unfamiliar man seated in front of me. To this day he probably thinks there was an absolute lunatic sitting behind him in church that morning. *Come to think of it, I never saw him again. I think I scared him off.* Every word of the readings, every prayer, and every song that day touched me more deeply than it ever had before, and I cried to the point of hyperventilating. People handed me kleenex and I was embarrassed because I didn't want to draw attention to myself, but I just couldn't stop crying. I couldn't think of a better place to be than at my church totally humbled in God's presence.

When it was time to walk forward for communion the usher approached my pew and looked at me apprehensively, wondering if he should extend help or just bypass me. I stood up and my legs felt like jello, but I was determined to receive communion that day. I was blubbering the entire way up to the front, trying to hide my face because, by this time, my make-up was smeared all over and I felt so foolish. I remember reaching the front and seeing friends of ours with tears in their eyes for Larry. As the pastor looked at me, his eyes welled up also. He turned to the person assisting him and handed them the bread he was about to give me. Then he did something I had never seen a minister do before. He gave me a hug and we sobbed together for a brief moment. Then he took the bread back and blessed me as he gave it to me. I could barely hold it in my mouth and breathing through my nose made my crying that much louder.

Upon returning to my seat, I remember people sitting around me that weren't there before. Several of my friends crowded around and were very supportive, but I just wanted to disappear. I never meant to make a scene and draw attention to myself.

After church, I sat in my car for several minutes, regrouping before

I went home. I thanked God for giving me the strength to be there that day, and I prayed that Larry would be with me the next time.

At home, I found Dina making breakfast for her dad and boyfriend, and things seemed to be going well. By their sad expressions, I knew they realized I had been crying a great deal. I got myself together and joined them for coffee. Shortly afterwards, Dina was on her way back to Madison. It was so hard to watch her leave.

"I love you dad and I'll call tomorrow night to see how things went. Keep your chin up," she advised him. Again, I saw her fighting back tears. "Love you mom. Stay strong."

So now, I thought about how all this would affect our day to day lives and realized that I had to let my employer know what was happening.

I was a registered nurse at a workshop for developmentally disabled adults, whom we referred to as "consumers." The facility also provided transportation for them throughout the county. We transported the consumers each day to and from work, and took some on outings or to medical appointments. About 80 consumers attended daily. There was so much to learn, so many behaviors to contend with, so many personalities and disorders to learn about. I loved my job, my co-workers, my supervisor and most of all, the consumers. I had only been there five months and was fearful that this kind of situation could jeopardize my position, my wages, and our health insurance. But my husband came first, and God would take care of everything else.

I telephoned my director at home to let him know what was going on, as it was imperative that I miss work the next day—and possibly many more days in the future. Being such a new employee, it frightened me to think of calling this man and telling him that I found it necessary to put my husband's health before my job. Not all employers

THE GIFT OF TODAY

understand in that situation. That was a telephone call I will long remember.

The moment he answered the phone and I began explaining what was going on, my voice started trembling and I could barely speak. He could hear the helplessness in my voice, and calmly told me, "If you are at all concerned about your job, Dianne, that's the least of your worries at this time. Your family will always come first here. You take as much time as you need to be with your husband. If you need two years off to take care of him, your job will be here for you when you return."

How many people can say that their employer has given them that kind of peace in a family emergency? He assured me that I would have nothing to worry about. And he was faithful to his word.

That night as Larry and I lay in bed, he told me that he felt a little better. But his voice was still quite raspy. We talked a little about our plans for going to the hospital the next day and tried to be as upbeat as possible. It would be a long day and we needed to be on top of our game. Larry fell fast asleep. I sat up, wide awake, and reminisced.

CHAPTER FOUR

Back to the Beginning

My thoughts took me back to a very different time. In some respects it seemed like a lifetime ago, and in others it seemed like yesterday.

It was 1975 and I had been living apart from my family for over two years. My roommate and I shared the same first name, and a two-bedroom apartment in a great complex in Hillside, Illinois. She was a pediatric nurse at the time and I worked for a large aluminum manufacturing company as a supervisor. (We are now both nurses).

It was a turbulent and controversial time. It was the age of mood rings, the floppy disc, long hair, tie-dyed shirts and torn jeans, mini skirts, and pop artists like Andy Warhol. Political and social unrest grew from U.S. participation in the Vietnam war, the Watergate controversy, and Roe v. Wade protests. It was definitely a man's world even though the United Nations had declared 1975 as "The Year of the Woman." I guess we should have figured out back then that the U.N. was in the dark. Women were still struggling to receive fair wages for the same job a man performed, and often times were not given the opportunity to fill a position previously held by a man.

The guys I knew all seemed so immature for their ages, didn't have their heads on straight, and wanted to party, smoke dope and drink.

THE GIFT OF TODAY

That just wasn't my idea of a good time. I was looking for someone who wasn't afraid to earn an honest living, could have a little fun without bringing excessive alcohol or drugs into the relationship, and used good judgment. What happened to the guys you see in the movies who could talk to their girls for hours about anything or nothing? Where were the guys who liked to get dressed up and go dancing; the guys who opened doors for their dates; the guys who liked to go to fine restaurants for candlelit dinners? I was totally convinced that there was no one in this world for me, and with that in mind, I had sworn off men.

About three months prior, I had ended a relationship that I thought was going to result in marriage. Fortunately for me, this particular guy showed his true colors before the relationship progressed any further.

I was meeting my dear friend Marie at the B&R Restaurant for supper, where she worked as a waitress. I had just come from my semi-annual dental check-up and had dazzling white teeth. I was wearing a very flattering dress and heels and having a good hair day.

As we chatted over dinner, a handsome guy that smelled as good as he looked came and sat beside me in the booth and began talking to Marie. He was dressed in a navy blue leather jacket, a denim western shirt, jeans and biker boots. The fragrance he was wearing along with the scent of leather was something I wanted to bottle and take home. After a few minutes of kibitzing, Marie introduced him to me as Larry. He seemed to have a pleasant personality and carried on quite a conversation. After inquiring about me, he said he knew Marie well as he was going through a divorce and was eating three meals a day at the restaurant.

He had thick black hair that lay almost perfectly and had a slight curl at the nape of his neck where it touched the back of his collar. He had a moustache and penetrating brown eyes. I remember making a couple comments that struck him funny and when he laughed his gold crowns gleamed. He had an inviting laugh that seemed so relaxed and there was nothing forced or phony about him. He was mature and seemed unaffected by his surroundings. He asked me to join him next door at the bar for a drink with Marie and her boyfriend Bill, who had now made this a foursome. I tried to excuse myself, but Marie convinced me to join them.

As we got up to leave the restaurant, Larry grabbed for my check. I let him know in no uncertain terms that I was not going to allow a stranger to pay for my dinner. He said he was just trying to be a gentleman and felt it would be the appropriate thing to do since he "barged in" during our supper. When he could see I was serious, I saw this look of intrigue and apprehension come over him.

The bar owner also owned the restaurant where Marie was employed, so she knew everyone there well. There were no tables available, so the four of us sat at the bar, where Marie and I were now separated by the two guys.

Larry and I got to know each other well and we had a great time together. Someone played a slow song, "Feelings," on the jukebox, and Larry asked me to dance. I was hesitant because I never felt relaxed enough to let a man lead when we danced, but he convinced me to let him try. It was so natural and I felt so relaxed in his arms. He kept talking to me and would occasionally sing the words to the song, and I made it through the entire dance without stepping on his toes. I insisted on leaving after that, and although he tried to talk me into staying, I think he felt it was better not to be too forward and scare me off. He asked if he could walk me to my car, and showed me his Honda in the parking lot on the way. He asked for my phone number and I told him I didn't feel I knew him well enough for that. Maybe we would bump into each other again sometime.

A couple days later, that's exactly what happened. Marie and I were visiting over coffee at the same restaurant and along came Larry. He

THE GIFT OF TODAY

joined us again, smelling as good as he did the first time I met him and looking equally as handsome. Before I knew it we were at the bar dancing to the song "Feelings" again. This time it was Larry that requested the song on the jukebox, and this time he held me much closer. There was such a comfort in having his arms around me; a comfort I had not felt with a man before.

One thing led to another, and soon I was writing down my phone number for Larry. He called the following evening, which happened to be a Friday. In the course of the conversation, which was going quite well, he asked me out for dinner and a movie the following evening. Larry learned about the wrath of a woman as I bluntly told him that I was not sitting around my apartment waiting for someone to ask me out for the following evening. I said that I already had plans and he would have to call a week in advance if he wanted to take me out. We ended our conversation shortly after that, and immediately the phone rang again. When I picked it up, it was Larry.

"Hi beautiful," he said, "Any chance of taking you to dinner and a movie NEXT Saturday evening?" I almost fell over. I thought sure that after a blasting like he had just received, I would never hear from him again. Not so. *How can you turn down an offer like that?*

Our first date was one I would never forget. He took me out for a very nice dinner and to see the movie, *The Way We Were* with Barbara Streisand and Robert Redford. It was my request. Halfway through the movie, I realized Larry had not only fallen asleep next to me but he started snoring in the movie theatre! I gave him a nudge with my elbow and he was so embarrassed and apologetic. I thought I was boring him, but the man was just exhausted from working so many hours. I guess in those days, this movie would have been considered a "chick flick." I thought sure this would be our one and only evening together, but he managed to win me over with a cup of coffee, that wonderful scent of leather combined with his cologne, and meaningful conversation after the movie. We just seemed to be able to talk about anything and I noticed he was a superb listener. He made great eye contact and really paid attention when I spoke. That meant a lot to me because it was a trait that had become so rare.

Our friendship blossomed into a serious relationship quickly as Larry's divorce was finalized. We survived a lot of harassment from Larry's ex-wife while we dated and after we were married. Some days were absolute torture, but we were determined to be together and not let anyone or anything interfere.

I remember the day I met Larry's youngest son, Don. I had actually met him about a year and a half earlier while dating another guy who played on a baseball team. We all gravitated to a particular bar after games for a drink. If my date and I got separated during the evening, I would yell, "Hey Don, give me a 301." That was a code between us in case the owner was around, that I wanted a drink and that my date would pay for it later. I never expected that when Larry took me into this bar it was to introduce me to his son, the bartender!

It was that day that I finally asked Larry how old he was. Until that time, I never gave it a real thought. When he said there was a twenty-five year difference in our ages, I couldn't believe I had fallen for someone that much older than me. There was a youthful spirit about Larry that defied his age so well. I have since come to the realization that age is merely a number. In this case, it was also an indication of maturity, stability and decency. That's not always the case.

We found ourselves comfortably fitting into a group of about 30 people ranging in ages from mid-twenties to mid-forties. We all had a great time together. As we approached Thanksgiving and Larry learned that my family was coming for dinner, he asked if he could meet them for the first time. I was so nervous about my folks meeting Larry, finding out we were dating, and the age difference between us. So I invited the whole gang of 30 friends for a dinner and most of them did come. We all mingled together and my parents met Larry,

THE GIFT OF TODAY

but didn't put us together as a couple. I remember asking him not to say anything that would give away his age until they had a chance to really get to know him. The next thing I knew, he and my dad were discussing the Korean War (in the first person), and I was kicking Larry under the table and changing the subject.

One of my favorite dates was the night we went to Drury Lane, a dinner club outside Chicago, for dinner and dancing with two co-workers and their wives. I wore a white pant outfit with a bare midriff partially hidden by long white fringe. Each time Larry looked at me, his eyes sparkled and he told me repeatedly that I was the most beautiful woman he'd ever known. We danced until our legs could barely hold us up anymore and I sang a song by Captain and Tenille with the band. Larry was mesmerized. I only wore that outfit one other time, but Larry talked about it for 25 years.

I remembered the night we invited Larry's best friend, Bill, to my apartment for dinner. Larry wanted to impress Bill and his girlfriend with my cooking, so he asked me to make them my famous beef stroganoff. I had probably made this dish 25 times or more and Larry loved it. That evening, for some strange reason that we never figured out, my sauce turned out pink. I kept thinking that surely it was going to change to a nice rich brown color as I stirred it, but it just stayed pink. Larry and I were both a bit panicky, but we served it anyway and it tasted terrible. Shortly after that, we found ourselves in a local restaurant ordering off the menu. I was so embarrassed. Larry never made me feel bad that night, but anytime an opportunity came up to tell a joke, he would bring up the night I made pink stroganoff to impress his best friends!

Then came Christmas. I had mentioned to my mom that I was interested in bringing Larry home with me for Christmas. My mom looked rather puzzled, and asked, "Doesn't he have family?" Not exactly the

Dianne Klancir

Christmas spirit I was hoping for! I explained that he did, but his kids were grown, they each had places to go, he had gone through a bitter divorce and really didn't have anyone to spend the holiday with. She was happy to include him if I wanted him there.

Larry asked me one evening when we were out shopping together to step into a Keepsake jewelry store with him. He walked me over to the wedding ring counter and watched my expression as I looked at the rings in the case.

"See anything you like in there?" he asked. I pointed to sets that included an engagement ring, wedding ring and groom's ring. There was one that especially caught my eye. Several days later, Larry proposed to me and I accepted. It was one of the happiest days of my life. What I didn't know was that he had gone back and bought those rings that I had admired in the jewelry store.

When we arrived at my parents' house for Christmas Eve, I told him that he was expected to ask my dad for my hand in marriage. He looked a little pale, but said that would be no problem. He tried numerous times to get my dad alone to speak to him, but it wasn't working out. Finally, my mom asked my dad to pick up something at the store before it closed, and Larry volunteered to go along. I went also, and when we got to the store I ran inside, leaving the two of them alone in the car to talk.

I didn't know what to expect and I peered through the store windows, watching to see if there was any pushing and shoving going on in the car, or if things seemed to be moving in a positive direction. I could tell there was a discussion taking place, and then it seemed that they both got very quiet and were each staring out their respective car windows.

When I returned to the car, I looked at them both, and asked, "So how's it going???"

Larry responded, "I asked your dad for your hand in marriage."

THE GIFT OF TODAY

"OH?" I said, "And what did you say, dad?"
"I need to discuss it with your mother," was his response. End of discussion. It was totally quiet the rest of the way home.

As we all busied ourselves getting ready for Christmas Eve dinner, I expected to see my dad take my mom off to the side and talk with her. We never witnessed the two of them alone together the entire day. Larry had brought two bottles of champagne for the occasion, and asked my dad if it would be appropriate to serve it with dinner. My father approved.

As we took our places at the table and said the blessing, my dad announced he was making a toast. We all raised our glasses as he announced, "I would like to welcome our future son-in-law to the family. Larry has asked for my blessing to marry Dianne today and I am giving it to him. Congratulations to the two of you."

My mother's expression changed from a grin to a weak smile and her arm dropped to the table. She was in total shock, as my dad had not said one word to prepare her for this. I knew she didn't feel at the time that this was the right person for me, but when she got to know Larry better, she really did like him.

In May, we purchased our first home together and on July 4th, 1976, we were married. It was a blowout wedding with fireworks, red, white and blue bridesmaid gowns, parades for the bicentennial celebration and the Lutheran minister who married us dressed in a three-pointed hat, cape and black knickers. The weather was perfect, my dress was exquisite, the flowers were incredible, and Larry's ex-wife was calling us threatening to destroy the ceremony and reception. We had the time of our lives and fortunately, the 'ex' never showed up. I didn't think I could ever be that happy. I cried through my vows and Larry always teased me that he wasn't sure if I actually ever said them or not.

As I thought about those vows, I remembered the words, *"from this day forward, for richer or poorer, in sickness and health, 'til death do us part."* I wondered if this was a test of those vows.

Most of all, that evening in 2001, I thought about the way Larry made me feel when he looked into my eyes, the way he held me in his arms, his strength, his laugh, his demeanor. Always the calming influence; always patient and kind. Those were the characteristics I had fallen in love with. I loved the way he used to say to me, "Pinch me so I know this is for real and you're not just in my dreams."

I had fallen asleep on the couch lost in my thoughts and memories. I remember waking up about 4:00 a.m. and dragging myself to bed. I snuggled up to Larry and he wrapped his arm around me almost automatically. I loved that feeling and I never wanted it to end. As I felt myself drifting off to sleep, my prayers began again.

"Lord, You have given me a terrific guy. I am not ready to give him up and I will fight for him until I have no fight left. I will honor my vows made to Larry and to You that I will love and cherish this man until the day that one of us physically leaves this earth. I thank You for the wonderful earthly life You have given us and I pray for forgiveness for anything I have done that was not pleasing to You. I ask You for strength for both of us to endure whatever is to come, for wisdom in making the correct decisions, for physicians who are dedicated and compassionate, and for friends and family to support us in this trying time. I ask these things in Your Son Jesus' holy name. Amen."

CHAPTER FIVE

The Longest Week of Our Lives

We woke up Monday morning full of optimism and hope.
   We contacted our family physician and faxed him the paper work the doctor at the walk-in clinic sent us home with. We explained that we were meeting with the pulmonologist that morning at her office in the ER.
   When we arrived, the emergency room was jammed with very sick respiratory patients, and I was not at all happy about Larry being around all that illness. We were totally unaware that, for two days, the hospital had been using the ER to admit and hold patients because all the regular hospital rooms were full. At least we were taken into an examining room immediately, where we patiently waited our turn to be seen.

   The pulmonologist was a wonderfully calm, compassionate woman whom my husband adored. She was beautiful to say the least with blonde hair like spun gold and glistening white teeth. She had a terrific bedside manner and Larry took to her like a fish to water. If she had said, "Jump!" he would have asked, "How high?" Anyway, that's the relationship I wanted him to have with his doctor because I knew we would get things accomplished.

Dianne Klancir

She immediately decided that Larry needed to be admitted, ordered sputum cultures, blood cultures, IV antibiotics, nebulizer treatments, and told us he would have to spend the night in the ER as no hospital rooms were available.

I approached the doctor with my concern about an advanced lung cancer patient having to spend the night in an emergency room with people who were coughing and had respiratory infections. I told her I would appreciate any strings she could pull to get Larry into a hospital room and away from the sickness that had infiltrated that area. Then I silently prayed for a room for my husband. About an hour later, he was taken to a room on the 4th floor. We had received our first miracle of the week.

Larry looked so depressed and was getting very winded with little effort. I brought in a pad of paper and pencil and asked him to conserve his voice by writing down what he wanted to say. Even then, sometimes I barely got a response from him when I asked a question. It seemed like he was giving up.

I think the anger about this disease hit me, and I just couldn't hold it in any longer. I lectured, "You know, Larry, I know this isn't my body and it isn't my tumor, but it might as well be. We are one and we have been for 25 years. Whatever affects you, deeply affects me. This is killing me that you won't talk to me and you are acting like the world has come to an end. Ninety percent of recovery from cancer is having the will to live and the right attitude. You have been strong all your life. Now that the real battle is here, are you going to surrender? You had better look that tiger in the eye and say, 'come and get me but you're in for the fight of your life!' I need you here with me. I'm not ready to let you go. God will give you the armor if you are ready for the fight. Are you prepared to go to battle, or am I an army of one here? I need to know!"

Larry looked at me in disbelief. He couldn't believe how upset I was.

THE GIFT OF TODAY

"Don't get mad, I just don't know if I can put you through all this. I don't want to be a burden to you," he responded as his lip quivered.

I immediately softened my tone and sobbed, "I'm not mad at you. I'm mad at this disease. You're not a burden to me. I love you with all my heart and I know that God will be watching over us, as He always has. I take care of total strangers, why wouldn't I want to take care of my husband? I need your promise that you will not give up until you have nothing left to give. Until that very moment, I won't give up either," I reassured him. He promised me he would try and that was all I could hope for. Tears streamed from our eyes and we caressed each other. I just never wanted to let go of him.

As I looked at him, I thought about the moments in our lives that made me fall so deeply and passionately in love with this man.

I remembered when we were dating and I spent hours making a cake for a friend of ours. As we were getting ready to leave, I accidentally laid the cover on the lettering on top of the cake and ruined it. I was so flustered. Larry held up his hand and motioned for me to sit down. He painstakingly took a toothpick and picked off each letter, then smoothed out the frosting, and allowed me to rewrite "Happy Birthday" on the cake.

Then there was the night we had been drinking wine at a party and I got sick in his car on the way home. I consumed alcohol very infrequently, and usually nursed one drink the entire evening. Drinking two glasses of wine that night literally put me over the edge. He never said a word. The next day he showed up with a sparkling clean vehicle and flowers for me, hoping I felt better.

I remembered having a bad case of pleurisy while I was renting a room from an elderly lady. I was so sick and there was no way to cook a meal where I lived. Larry brought me soup and sat with me until I fell asleep.

I remembered when he surprised me with my engagement ring on Christmas Eve after my dad had given us his blessing. He had it wrapped in this large, beautifully wrapped box under the tree. When I opened it and realized he had gone back and purchased the ring set I had admired, I was blown away. He wouldn't even let me pay for his ring.

I remembered staying out until 2:00 a.m. on dates with him and then meeting him at 6:30 a.m. for breakfast at the restaurant where we met. We both wore sunglasses so no one could see the big black rings under our eyes from lack of sleep. We looked like lovesick raccoons. There he would be, waiting with a smile for me each time.

Then there was the day about a year-and-a-half after we were married that I came home and told him that I was pregnant. We had been trying such a short time to conceive and we were both shocked when it happened so quickly. He was ecstatic. A few months later, he was busy making a cradle for our new addition to the family. I came home from my doctor appointment and nervously informed him that we could possibly be having twins. I was a little concerned that he might be upset, but instead, his eyes got like saucers, he picked up his keys and headed for the door. I thought, in my emotional pregnant state that he was going to walk out on me, and I tearfully asked, "Where are you going?" He exclaimed, "I'm going to the lumber yard to get more wood. We're going to need two cradles!" I didn't know if I should laugh or cry, but I knew that I loved him for that. I told him that we should hold off until we knew the results for sure, and as it turned out, there was only one beautiful baby.

I felt so lucky to have found the guy I had been looking so desperately for. Without a doubt, 1975 WAS the year for THIS woman!

Finally, I laid back in the chair and fell asleep so that he could rest. I spent the night in his hospital room because I couldn't get myself to leave, and the entire time we held hands through the bedrails. Tomorrow would be another full day.

On Tuesday, February 20, the pulmonologist met us in Larry's

THE GIFT OF TODAY

hospital room to say that she would not confirm the diagnosis we had previously received until her tests were completed.

Larry continued to run a low-grade temperature and cough up blood. He had more chest x-rays that morning. In comparison to his x-ray on Saturday, there was already a change indicating that his breathing was being done almost entirely by the right lung. His pulse oximetry (oxygen saturation level) at rest was 96-97%, which is totally amazing. And, after a six-minute walk in the hallway, it never dipped under 91%. His right lung was working like a racehorse, but it was comforting to know that it could handle the job. He had not yet needed oxygen. (Miracle number two.)

Larry coughed up blood all morning and complained of heaviness in his chest. About 12:00, I called his oldest son, Les, whom we had not seen in quite some time. I explained what was happening and he insisted on coming to the hospital to see his dad. He and his wife, Judy, and daughter, Abby, lived in a Chicago suburb, about two hours away. Les, in turn, contacted his brother and sister to tell them about their dad.

At 3:00, Larry had a CAT scan of his lungs. At 4:00 he received a call from his youngest son, Don, whom Larry had not heard from in several years. (Miracle number three.)

At 4:15, our pastor (bless his wonderful heart) brought communion and anointing oil. Two of our friends were present and they received the sacrament also. By 4:30, 16 more of our friends had filled the room, including another pastor. We all gathered around Larry's bed and held a brief prayer/annointing service as we held hands. Larry was moved to tears at the outpouring of love and Christian spirit in the room. It was a life-changing moment for both of us.

From that point on, Larry's entire demeanor changed. He perked up and was prepared to do battle with this disease. He ate a decent supper for the first time in two days. In the meantime, three more friends appeared. He was so encouraged that day. He couldn't talk because he got so winded but he appreciated the company very much. Larry was always a better listener than talker anyway.

Larry's son and daughter-in-law arrived and insisted on taking me to dinner to get me out of that hospital room for a while. They stayed in Rockford overnight so that they could return again to see Larry in the morning.

As I left the hospital that evening, I received a wonderful surprise. For the first time in two days, Larry's coughing did not produce blood. His sputum was clear and he spoke one full sentence without getting short-winded. His color was improved from that morning and he was in much better spirits. Everything was pointing in a very positive direction. He smiled several times and told me how much he loved me repeatedly.

The next day Larry was to receive a definitive diagnosis. The CAT scan results would be back, and the doctor was anticipating having to remove some of the fluid surrounding his lungs to have it analyzed. We discussed life and death issues that we needed to address that night and we both felt better than we had in days.

Truly, we had the most wonderful friends in the world. Having family such a long distance away sure made a person appreciate those who were close by at a time like that. We also had the most wonderful employers. We had been blessed in so many ways. We learned the importance of turning this over to God and letting him carry the burden. It was far too much for any human to handle alone. "NO BURDEN IS TOO HEAVY FOR GOD'S ALMIGHTY ARMS. When life becomes too exhausting, remember Jesus offers rest for your soul." (Matthew 11:28-30).

Wednesday, February 21, 2001, began by getting the results of Larry's CAT scan. The pulmonologist carefully identified everything on the scan so that Larry and I understood what we were looking at.

THE GIFT OF TODAY

It was incredible to see those lungs on a CAT scan and see the difference between a normal and abnormal lung. The left lung was almost completely compressed now due to the fluid in the pleural space, and the tumor pressing against his bronchus was a little over 9cm. (about 4 inches). There was also another tumor (smaller, about 6 cm) that was wrapped around his pulmonary artery and aorta.

She confirmed that this was definitely lung cancer. Yet, somehow when she said it that day, it wasn't quite as devastating. We were more peaceful and ready to deal with this in whatever way was necessary. The initial shock was over and I truly believe that the anointing service with our friends gave us an incredible sense of strength and peace.

The pulmonologist took him away to remove the fluid build up in the pleural cavity. Larry handled the procedure like a champion. She removed 2-1/2 liters of fluid, very dark red in color—normally, pleural fluid is the color of straw. That was an unbelievable amount of fluid, in a color we didn't want to see, and was sent to the laboratory to determine the type of cancer.

All that fluid had been pressing against his lung and tumor, causing him to be short of breath. As the lung re-expanded, he began to have pain across his chest and up his shoulder. The pulmonologist ordered pain medication and after the first dose, he felt like a new person. What a trooper! As soon as Les and Judy knew he was alright, they returned home. But it meant so much to Larry that they were there with him.

The doctor ordered a bone scan for the following day and a visit with the oncologist she recommended to discuss our options. We were bracing ourselves for what might be coming, but with God's grace we were feeling strong and up for the task. Larry's color began returning to his face after awhile and he was able to talk to friends on the phone without getting too winded. He even laughed a few times.

Larry received several phone calls and visitors in addition to flowers that day. It meant so much that people cared so deeply, and I could see how his spirits were lifted every time another call came or another person arrived to visit.

Our friends Dave and Eleanor insisted on having dinner with me at the end of their visit because they knew that I wasn't eating at the hospital. There's not much joy in eating a meal alone in a hospital cafeteria. It was so good to eat something besides hospital food. My prayer was that God would bless our friends, relatives and doctors for their loving work and generous spirit. We were so touched by the outpouring of affection.

Thursday almost drove both of us crazy. It was long and boring because nothing seemed to be happening very quickly. (Sounds like the Army...hurry up and wait).

They came to get Larry hurriedly that morning for his bone scan, which was a breeze because he just laid on a table and the dye they injected into his veins did the work. The rest of the day we sat and waited for doctors to appear with test results.

We played cards, opened mail and circled words in puzzle books. I read to him, we took two walks in the hallway—anything to keep our minds busy. I stayed in that room all day until I finally decided to go to the cafeteria and force down some supper. As soon as I was seated at the table with my dinner tray, I was paged to my husband's room. The doctor had arrived. *Figures.* No supper that night, but that was the least of my concerns. This was the visit I had waited for.

The pulmonologist informed us that the cancer type was "non-small cell." That was good news. That was the less aggressive type. However, so far they knew it was in the lung and pleural fluid. She said they would probably still have to do a bronchoscopy and biopsy to determine if other types were present. The liver was clear on the CAT scan and the left adrenal gland (above the kidney) showed thickening, but she was not concerned at that point about it. That was our good news.

THE GIFT OF TODAY

The not-so-good news was that the oncologist we had chosen left a message for us that he could not take Larry's case because he was leaving the following morning for a two-week vacation. That left two other oncologists to choose from, both female, and one was Croatian. (That was Larry's nationality. Guess who he picked!) So, we waited another day to see an oncologist because it was now after 6:00 p.m.

In the meantime, I requested a private room for my husband and told the doctor we would pay the difference the insurance didn't cover. The man Larry shared a room with was coughing productively, snored all night and would loudly yell out. Every time they brought my husband's meal tray, that man started a coughing jag that completely took away Larry's appetite. A cancer patient should not be exposed to "who knows what" in the next bed. The doctor agreed and the process began. There were no open beds on the Oncology floor, but within an hour, my husband was moved into a private room and he had his best night's sleep in a week. I was able to go home knowing he would be rested.

There was talk of a possible brain scan that week also because that would be the other area of likely cancer development (metastases). So far the news we received was news we could live with.

We were encouraged and thankful for all our good medical care. It was incredible to me how much advocating a spouse needed to do. I often wondered what happened to those people who had no medical background or just accepted whatever was told to them.

Each day I would strip my husband's bed, help him bathe from head to toe, assist with proper placement of his meal tray so that he could reach everything, reset his I.V. when it would start beeping, walk him in the hallways and give him a couple backrubs. As a former hospital nurse, I remembered how important those were to the patient and the nurses just didn't have time for that level of care. I kept track of his fluid intake and output, his I.V. site, and made sure he had a way to communicate with staff. They often thanked me for taking care of my husband the way I did and not getting upset with them for not having the time to do those things. I remembered what it was like to have eight or nine patients to attend to on a shift, and I was grateful to have something to do to pass the time. It was my privilege to take care of my husband the way I had taken care of so many others.

Friday morning Larry was taken for a bronchoscopy. That was a rather unpleasant procedure, but he was sedated throughout all but the end of it. He remembered very little. They put a little scope with a camera down his main breathing tube and looked at the inside of both lungs, took pictures and biopsies. The biopsies were very small and the pulmonologist wasn't quite sure they would be of much benefit, but they found out during the procedure that the tumor was not compressing the artery. It was attached to the bronchus and each time they touched that, it would start bleeding again. It wasn't a huge amount and it stopped right away, but that was why he was high risk for surgery. The other reason surgery could not be done was because it had already invaded the pleural space and fluid. Final diagnosis today: Stage IV (very advanced) non-small cell lung cancer.

We explored the options for treatment with the oncologist and made our decisions. I told Larry I would support whatever he decided to do. We pressed the oncologist for a timeline feeling it was only fair to have some idea of how much time a person had to prepare for the end of their life, with or without treatment. She said that with treatment, Larry would have about 18 to 23 months, at best. Knowing that chemo and radiation can be less than quality of life times, I left the decision totally up to Larry and told him I would stand beside him no matter what he decided. He chose to move forward with the treatment. I was elated. God had given him the strength to look that tiger square in the eye and we were on our way, full steam ahead.

We were told to go home and rest over the weekend. On Monday, Larry was to meet with the oncologist and begin chemo.

I asked, "Why chemo first and not radiation?" to which the oncol-

THE GIFT OF TODAY

ogist replied that they needed to get the chemo started as soon as possible to keep the fluid from returning. Until he received chemo, the fluid would keep coming back. If they had to keep drawing that fluid off, he would have developed scar tissue at those sites. After awhile, they would not be able to rid his body of any more fluid. The radiation would come later.

Larry was on an emotional roller coaster that day—first upbeat, then very down. I couldn't even begin to imagine what he was feeling. I only knew that from where I stood it was terrible, and it was difficult to be the one to remain upbeat and positive in the face of treatment we knew nothing about. I kept saying "Everything is going to be okay" or "Don't be afraid, we're in God's hands and we'll be fine." We learned to focus on one day at a time and one procedure at a time. We were so grateful for the care we had received thus far.

I believed in my heart that Larry had the fight in him now to beat this and that he would live well past the timeline the doctor had given him. He was a strong individual and he had things he wanted to do yet. For example, we needed to get his golf cart tuned up so that when the course opened in late April he was out there ready to play. That would be just the right medicine to keep him motivated!

Our friends, Dave and Eleanor helped us make it through a very difficult, exhausting week. They looked in on our dog, Molly, sent meals to the house, and arrived at the hospital just in time to load their vehicle with flowers and gifts Larry had received. They were so awesome. By the time we reached home, Larry was so exhausted he had just enough strength to make it to the chair and fell sound asleep. I asked God to continue to strengthen our faith, to bless us, and to take special care of our friends and relatives who were so uplifting. It's times like these that you know how precious your friends really are.

Dianne Klancir

It felt so good to be back in our own home, and our own bed. We slept like babies knowing we had made it through a rough week and survived. There were rocky roads ahead, but we were prepared to deal with them, one at a time. And best of all, we knew that God was in control and we were fine with that for the first time in our lives.

CHAPTER SIX

Angels at Work

We made it through a relaxing weekend without too much difficulty. Larry only required one pain pill that entire weekend and then he slept peacefully. He was using his inhalers and we checked his peak flow about four times per day. Each time the results improved, so we were hopeful.

Larry didn't feel like doing much on Saturday until Dina arrived. Since she was there with him, I left for a few minutes to run some errands. When I returned, her car was gone. I raced into the house thinking some emergency had occurred and she had to leave in a hurry. They were both gone with not a word as to their whereabouts. I couldn't figure out what happened to them. About fifteen minutes later, they pulled up in the driveway laughing and having the best time together. She had taken him for a ride in her little sporty car with the moon roof open, and they were having a ball. It was exactly what Larry needed. His spirits improved that entire day. Unfortunately, she did have to go back home and the goodbyes were always so difficult.

Sunday was quiet and uneventful. The following morning we were to start chemo treatments and neither of us was exactly sure of what to expect. The thought of putting poison into my husband's veins to make him better seemed like an oxymoron. But the doctors felt this was the best plan, and Larry was resolved to move forward with this treatment. I trusted that God would be there to oversee everything and I felt His closeness. We would do this together and somehow manage to stay positive and keep a sense of humor through it. I told Larry I was bringing uplifting stories and humorous anecdotes to remind us to stay focused and upbeat. As we climbed into bed that evening, I prayed:

"Lord, tomorrow is the first day of the rest of our lives. Make it a day filled with hope. Help us to focus on what we CAN do, rather than what we CANNOT. Help us learn to take one day at a time and to put our faith in You. Thank you for a week of answers, a week of wonderful medical care, and the angels that have come to us in the form of friends. We ask for Your continued blessings in Jesus' name. Amen."

The next morning before we left for the hospital in Rockford, I drove to work to get my paycheck. To my surprise, when I arrived at my desk, there was an envelope there with my name on it. When I opened it, there was over $200 cash inside a card signed by some of my co-workers. It stated, "Use this to help meet expenses while you are at the hospital for treatments and know that we are thinking of you and love you." I began to cry when I realized how incredible these co-workers of mine were and how fortunate I was to know each of them. Then I opened the envelope with my paycheck in it, and there were two checks inside. The other one was made out to me, but it was for a full two weeks pay of one of my co-workers. She had made arrangements with our accountant to turn over her last two weeks pay to me anonymously.

I had never experienced such generosity in my life! I sobbed out loud and again thanked God for bringing these tremendous people to me. However, I knew that in good conscience I could not keep someone's paycheck. Larry and I were not destitute by any means, and at that time I couldn't justify keeping the gift. I wrote the following note and handed it back to the company accountant with the paycheck:

THE GIFT OF TODAY

*Dear Angel of Finances and all that is good,
I am not sure who you are, but just to know that I work in the same building with you is an honor. Your generosity deeply touched me and I was moved to tears. However, I cannot accept your generous gift. At this time, Larry and I are financially stable, and it would be unfair for us to keep this. I do wish to thank you for your love and friendship, and I can only pray that someday we have the opportunity to return a favor to you, whoever you are. Blessings and peace, Dianne (& Larry too)*

Larry and I were in awe that someone who knew me for such a short time would perform such an unselfish, charitable act. We will never forget those generous gifts that people blessed us with at a time when expenses were mounting, but all we could think about was making it through the next treatment. Before long, Larry and I were on our way to the hospital filled with positive thoughts and a faith stronger than we had ever experienced. We were feeling quite unstoppable.

We met briefly with the oncologist at 9:00 a.m. who explained the plan of attack. Larry would be pre-medicated with a drug to stop the production of acid in his stomach, and one to prevent nausea. He would then begin his chemo treatment of Taxol®, which had numerous side effects, but whose benefits outweighed its risks. This would be followed by Carboplatinum. The two drugs would take a total of four and one-half hours to drip in through the I.V. line.

Larry and I were taken to a small room with a hospital bed, a recliner chair, a bedside table and a TV with VCR. This was to be our home for the day. We shifted things around to make ourselves comfortable, chose a video (which my husband made clear, we could only play after *The Price Is Right* TV show had aired), and we were set to go. As the nurse searched Larry's arm for the I.V. site to instill the poison, I began to feel nauseated. We realized these drugs were going to kill more than the cancer cells in my husband's body. I knew he was in for some rough days ahead—loss of appetite, body hair, libido; a feeling of overall weakness -- just to name a few of the side-effects. It felt like the room was getting smaller and I was having trouble getting air. In all my years of nursing, this had never happened to me before. I stepped out of the room for a minute and took a deep breath. I wiped away the tears that had rolled out the corners of my eyes and took another breath. I felt the color come back into my face and felt I could return. Larry was lying comfortably talking with the nurse, and they were laughing at a TV talk show.

When the nurse stepped out, I sat down beside him and stroked his arm. He squeezed my hand and we smiled at each other. He looked so much better than he did a week ago, and said he felt great even though his voice was still strained. He started to doze off and I tried to waken him when *The Price Is Right* came on, but he was just too tired to watch it.

As I sat holding Larry's hand and staring at him, I remembered times over the years when we fought, and what a waste of our time that was. *Why did we spend our time so foolishly? Why didn't we treasure the time we had been given here together rather than waste it on ridiculous things like who was right and who was wrong? Why did it seem that we were competing at times instead of being on the same team? Why were there times we didn't present a united front when we disciplined our daughter? Where were our priorities? Why were other things more important sometimes than each other?*

It's amazing how a serious illness can put things into perspective. The things that seemed so important to us previously, seemed so inconsequential now. I remembered thinking that it really mattered how nice a home we had or how much our income was. I remembered thinking that it was important that our daughter was one of the best dressed kids at school or that she was academically at the top of her

THE GIFT OF TODAY

class. How utterly ridiculous!! <u>Lesson: God loves us for who we are, not for what we have or what status we have attained.</u>

I also remembered how frustrated I became sometimes when Dina needed to be disciplined and Larry would ignore the responsibility. I thought about the times that he let things build to the point of boiling over, and then finally blurted out some punishment that totally exceeded the severity of the crime, and needed me to bail him out. For awhile; these things were happening repeatedly.

One day, I had finally reached the breaking point when Dina had an extremely inappropriate behavior and he pretended to look the other way. I was livid. It was exhausting being the one that had to straighten behaviors out and administer the punishment. I was always the bad guy and he was always in her good graces.

Larry's response to me was, "Well, she has always liked you better. She doesn't like me."

"This is not a popularity contest. You are her father," I retorted. "She looks to you for discipline. You can be her friend when she's older. Right now you need to show her that you are in control here. If you think she likes me more, it's because she knows what to expect from me. She knows that when she does something wrong, she'll be disciplined for it and the punishment will suit the crime. She never knows what to expect from you."

Unfortunately, this discussion took place in front of our daughter, and that should never have happened. After several more remarks back and forth, I headed to the bedroom with my suitcase and one for my daughter. It had gotten old playing both mother and father to Dina, and I decided that if I had to play both roles, I would do it alone. Larry didn't believe that I was actually leaving. He tried to talk to me then, but the time for that had passed, as I had tried to correct this for months. It was not getting better, it was getting worse.

I packed quickly, grabbed Dina by the hand and walked out the door. I took one last look back at the house to see Larry standing in the front window with tears in his eyes as we left. I was so frustrated and I had no idea where I was going to go. My parents lived next door and my sister lived about a mile away, but I needed to get farther away than that.

I got into the car with my daughter, who was about six years old at the time, and left. I cried and sobbed in the car as I drove. My daughter was full of questions, and I wanted to answer them all, but I had no answers. She wanted to know where we were going, why daddy wasn't with us, when she would see her dog again, and why mom and dad were so mad. I felt terrible. I knew it wasn't the right way to handle this, but I was at the end of my rope. I drove about 15 miles and pulled into a department store parking lot. I sat there for a minute and wiped away my tears. My daughter was in the back seat continuing to say, "Can't I go back to my dad and my dog?"

We went into the store so I could use the pay phone. I decided to call Larry and tell him not to discuss this with my parents until I had the chance to talk with them. When he answered, I could tell he'd been crying. He pleaded with me to come home and talk this out. I refused at first, but as he talked more and admitted he would try harder, I was convinced that going back was the right thing to do. We had to talk about this in a civil manner. He just didn't believe I was frustrated to the point of leaving. He was a good husband and father, he just didn't know how to be the disciplinarian.

In the meantime, Dina was standing in the store telling people that her mom took her away from dad and her dog and wouldn't take her back home. I was beginning to get strange looks from people in the store. I just wanted to work this out and take our daughter home. She was scared and I didn't mean to do that to her.

Larry and I talked for hours and worked out a solution that we could both live with. We explained to Dina that these were going to be the new rules at our house. She was so happy to be home. Yet, I can't help but think that this sad day haunted Dina for a long time. I regretted having to resort to leaving, but we had finally resolved the issue. From that point on, it improved. There were still times that it

THE GIFT OF TODAY

was far from perfect, but at least I saw effort on his part to share more of the discipline and do it appropriately.

It was one of two times in the 25 years we had been married that I left Larry for a very short time. We were never apart from each other overnight as a result of an argument. I don't believe we could have done that. But all arguments seemed so foolish now. How immature we were to fight rather than discuss these matters when God had so richly blessed us. Too often in the midst of fights, words are exchanged that are hurtful and cannot be retracted. They leave emotional scars. How thankful we should have been and how gracious God was to give us second chances.

I was far away in my thoughts when I suddenly realized that the nurse was addressing me. She was a kind, compassionate young girl, very committed to her patients. She asked if there was anything she could do for Larry or me. I told her we were fine, and that I was so glad he was resting. My eyes were full of tears from the place in my past I had just revisited, so she asked if I was alright. I told her I had just remembered a time in my past that I wished Larry and I would have been mature enough to handle differently.

"That happens frequently here," she whispered. "We cannot change the past, but we can do things differently today and tomorrow. Try to let go of past mistakes. God has already forgiven you for them, so use your energy in a more positive way. You need your strength right now. Stay focused on today. You two make a great team." Then she handed me a piece of paper with the following words on it:

"Cancer is so limited...
It cannot cripple Love
It cannot shatter Hope
It cannot corrode Faith
It cannot destroy Peace,
It cannot kill Friendship

Dianne Klancir

It cannot suppress Memories
It cannot silence Courage
It cannot invade the Soul
It cannot steal eternal Life
It cannot conquer the Spirit
If an incurable disease has invaded your life,
refuse to let it touch your spirit. Your body
can be severely afflicted and you may have a
great struggle. If you keep trusting God's
love, your spirit will remain strong.

I'm following Jesus,
One step at a time;
I live for the moment,
In His love divine.
Why think of tomorrow,
Just live for today;
I'm following Jesus,
Each step of the way.
The pathway is narrow,
But He leads me on;
I walk in His shadow,
My fears are all gone.
My spirit grows stronger,
Each moment, each day,
For Jesus is leading
EACH STEP OF THE WAY."
(anonymous)

I was so grateful for her words. We gave each other a warm hug and I felt like I had been touched by an angel.

I brought our lunch in a cooler that day. I set the bedside table and woke Larry up to eat. The nap did him a world of good. He ate a

THE GIFT OF TODAY

decent amount and felt rested. We watched the video, *While You Were Sleeping* and laughed out loud. It was unbelievable to me that while this horrible medicine was infiltrating my husband's body, he was able to laugh at a movie. Humor is such a vital part of recuperation from an illness. I had brought several humorous anecdotes from magazines and the internet. As I read them to him sometimes he would just smile. Other times he would let out a belly laugh that could be heard in the next room. It was music to my ears.

After a long, emotionally exhausting day, it was 5:00 p.m. and we were getting ready to leave the hospital. Larry's first treatment was complete, and the next couple days would tell whether or not he would have negative reactions to the medications. I silently prayed and asked God to help him tolerate the medicine without serious side effects. He was to return in three weeks for his next treatment if all went well. The doctor had anticipated he would need six to eight treatments.

Larry slept through the night and went the following day without a pain pill. He ate a huge plate of pancakes for breakfast that morning and began talking about his "things to do" list. I informed him that chemo patients are a little more fragile, and need to be protected from the public and people with coughs and colds. We would be avoiding smoke-filled rooms, crowded places, and going out in the cold weather. I discussed with him whether or not he felt I should go to work for a half-day, and he agreed it would be a good idea. The dog was there to keep him company, and I was only ten minutes away.

The next day, I stayed home because the nurses warned us that day three of chemo would be the worst. We anticipated it would be a good day that we could enjoy together. I asked if he would like to get a haircut, thinking that when his hair began falling out from the chemo it wouldn't be so devastating. He chose to wait until the following week. I couldn't blame him.

Dianne Klancir

He seemed less winded that morning and was in good spirits. He tolerated all the foods I served him for breakfast and against my better judgment, wanted to try "an outing." I bundled him up and took him to the nursing home where he worked to see all his buddies.

I sat him in a wheelchair when we arrived and strategically located him in the activity room, so that everyone who wanted to visit came to him (to conserve his strength). He chatted with so many friends, and those that were slightly under the weather exercised good judgment and stayed out of the room, but sent their best wishes. Everyone made him feel so welcome and was warm and uplifting. It was such a good experience—laughing, smiling and joking around, lots of hugs and a few tears.

We made a brief stop at the grocery store and he insisted on pushing the cart, which he always had. As I watched him, my thoughts took me to the times when we were walking through the grocery store and he would start dancing with the cart. He always enjoyed the easy listening music they played in the store. Now, how many people do you know that even pay attention to that music? The first few times I looked back to place something in the cart and saw him singing and swaying, I couldn't believe it. I couldn't help but smile, but asked, "Will you stop it? People are looking at us like we're crazy."

When I thought about it later, I had to admit it was pretty special that my husband was such a happy guy that the overhead music in the grocery store sent his feet into motion, and he wasn't embarrassed or self-conscious about it at all. Why was I? How come I wasn't that playful? I remembered how on several occasions he actually grabbed me in the store and we danced in the aisles.

One particular day, the guidance counselor from the high school our daughter attended, happened to be walking by the aisle. When he saw us, he laughed and yelled, "You two need to get out more so you don't have to dance in the grocery store. I never even realized

THE GIFT OF TODAY

there was music playing in here before. I wish I had a camera." Larry thought it was terribly humorous.

Unfortunately, he wouldn't be dancing today. And for the first time, I wished that he could have. By the time we got home, he was absolutely worn out.

To keep his iron count stable, without raising his platelets, we loaded up on apricots, raisins and beef liver. We hadn't had beef liver in years. Larry loved the way I prepared it, with grilled onions and bacon. Seeing as how he had a total cholesterol level of 150, I felt he could survive a little beef liver with bacon.

About mid-day he needed a couple Tylenol® due to some discomfort. By 10:00 p.m. he needed a stronger pain pill. That was the first time he had taken any painkillers since chemo on Monday.

Since Larry had slept well, I decided to go to work the following day. He seemed a little apprehensive about my leaving, asking me to check him for a fever and stating he wasn't sure he was okay. But, he was fine—just nervous about me being gone the entire day. His good friend Earl was coming for lunch so he wouldn't be alone for long. I provided the food so that all they had to do was sit, eat, and have a great time together, which they did.

Earl brought Larry an article from a local newspaper about a luncheon for cancer survivors on March 20th. It was free to cancer patients and a guest but they needed to make a reservation with the Country Club. Earl volunteered to go as Larry's guest if he would agree to attend. It was so kind of him, and after some hesitation, Larry responded that he would be honored to attend. He felt it was premature to consider himself a "cancer survivor" but said he could hear my voice in the background saying, "be positive".

My sister, Margie, whom Larry rarely saw, came for lunch and a visit the following day while I was at work. When my sister brought in the mail, he couldn't believe it. There were handfuls of cards. The florist also delivered a beautiful plant from the Lions Club that day. He received several phone calls and although he couldn't talk for long, he enjoyed listening to others and knowing that they cared enough to call. Everyone was being so supportive.

That evening I tried to take him for a drive. He insisted that he wanted to sit on the couch and watch TV. "I'm not ready for that today," he stated.

I didn't want to push too hard, but I knew that fresh air and seeing people (who were healthy) was good for him. The doctor told him he could do anything as long as he tolerated the chemo so well. He promised to go the Christian men's breakfast the following morning. Larry had assisted with that breakfast for a few years. He would make pancakes, steak and eggs, french toast, or whatever they needed, for as many as 80 men during each Saturday in Lent. He enjoyed the fellowship and loved having control of a kitchen (at home, the kitchen was my domain).

When the morning rolled around, he seemed more short of breath again, and decided he was too tired to participate. I wanted to insist, but thought better of it. He knew what he could tolerate, and I wanted him to know I had confidence in his decision.

He had more well-wishers bearing food and greetings that afternoon and watched a favorite video. I prayed to God that evening as we retired,

"*Lord, You have been so good and so patient with us. You have showered us with your Grace and I thank You for that. There were times we didn't find much time for You in our lives. You waited and knew we would find You again. How selfish of us to be so involved in our own lives that we didn't place You as our priority. Here I am again, selfishly asking that You inspire my husband to desire more than these four walls. Please help him to see the beauty of those around him who want so badly for him to be whole again, in body,*

THE GIFT OF TODAY

mind and spirit. I am in awe of Your unconditional love for us. Please forgive me for those times when I overlooked the beauty of Your creation, the wonder of Your being and the loving arms You placed around us to protect us. I pray that You will continue to bless our family and give us renewed strength through Your grace. In Jesus' name, Amen."

    Larry had six hours of uninterrupted sleep that night and woke the next morning with improved color and a better outlook. We went to church together and he even insisted on driving. We sat near the front of the church so he wouldn't have to walk so far for communion. He even went to the fellowship hall for coffee and a short visit with our church family afterward. Everyone rallied around him and made him feel so loved. We rested the afternoon away, enjoying the peace and comfort of our home and each other.

    That evening we were invited to the home of our friends Dick and Diane for dinner. Dick was one of Larry's co-workers and a great admirer of my husband's courage and strength. They set a beautiful table with their best china, candles and silver. Dick made a wonderful warm rice pudding heavily laced with cinnamon, and Diane outdid herself with the meat entrée and vegetables. Larry ate better than he had in two weeks and it was so wonderful to see him interact so positively. It was a very special evening with very special friends.

    Dina called that evening to say that she was coming home on Wednesday after work. That kept him motivated the entire week!

    The next morning (Monday), after another great nights sleep, Larry awakened with a positive attitude and enthusiasm that I hadn't seen in months. I attributed it to the great company he and I shared the evening before and God answering my prayers. He insisted I go to work and even volunteered to drive me. He said he would take himself to the local clinic for his blood work. I didn't argue. It was such a blessing to see him that way.

Dianne Klancir

He was so motivated that for the first time in a week, he wore something other than a jogging suit. He put on jeans, a shirt and tennis shoes. When he arrived at the end of the day to pick me up, he was greeted with another surprise. One of my co-workers had made him a container of hand-cranked, homemade ice cream. It was butter pecan, my husband's favorite! He looked like the cat that swallowed the canary as he ate that, and you could see the visions in his head of days gone by when he made homemade ice cream as a kid. He savored every bite.

The next day he insisted on taking the car for an oil change and the dog to the groomer. It was wonderful for me that he had this level of energy. I was able to go to work and not have to run errands afterwards. We could spend the evening together at home talking, sharing and enjoying our fireplace.

Our friends, Diane and Bill, and another close friend also named Bill, called that evening and asked if they could come out the following weekend. Both guys were in our wedding party, one of them being the best man. They lived two hours away and we rarely got together. It was the kind of friendship that no matter how long it had been since we had spoken or seen each other, we could pick right back up where we left off, seemingly without missing a beat.

I don't know if people realized how important it was to us that these phone calls were received. They were so motivating for Larry and me and kept us focused on the positive things happening in our lives. God surrounded us with angels everywhere we went and blessed us continuously. I knew my husband well enough to know that some days he wanted to just sit in front of the TV. While he needed his rest, it was not in his best interest to spend days in brainless activity. He always felt better when he had a project or event to motivate him. Let's face it, everyone feels better when they have a reason to get up in the morning.

THE GIFT OF TODAY

The following day was the best yet. Larry's blood test results were back, and his hemoglobin had only dropped two-tenths of one point. *Hallelujah!* His white cell count dropped more dramatically because of the chemo, but they were high to begin with because of the pneumonia. So all in all, everything was wonderful. Thank God for liver, apricots and raisins! That evening we ate sausage lentil soup, which was also a great source of iron.

Larry took our car in for new brakes and while he waited in the showroom, a lady approached him and told him of her inoperable thyroid tumor. He came home with incredible stories of her illness, and told me how he asked God to give her strength. I thought he would have been bored all those hours waiting, but he came home inspired and had witnessed to another person.

The biggest surprise was when he took his cap off. He had gone to the barber for his haircut. He made the decision to get a buzz cut. Talk about "shock and awe." He went alone and had his beautiful black and silver hair skimmed right off. Hair loss can be such a difficult thing for some men to handle, but he knew it would be falling out and thought it would be easier to handle if it was shorter. I was so proud of him for doing that. When he told the barber he was going through chemo, the barber gave him the cut at no charge. How wonderful was that?

He went to the bowling alley the next morning to visit some of his senior buddies and came home with his favorite pie, a coconut cream, which our good friend Eleanor had made. He purred through every bite of that over the next several days.

Dina arrived with a basketful of treats that the tenants in her building had put together for her to snack on during her trips home to see her dad. Angels again!

During her visit, we decided that Larry's new nicknames would either be Mr. Clean, Yul (Brenner, from *The King and I*) or Telly

(Savalas, from *Kojak*). All of them had bald heads and their own style. We either needed to get him a bag of suckers or an earring. We hadn't decided which yet.

We also learned something important these last two weeks. <u>Lesson: Our greatest enemy was not disease, it was despair.</u>

When we took the time to see the positives around us and not give in to the negatives, there was so much to be grateful for. We learned to keep the faith, to have happy hearts and to never give up hope. I thanked God for those angels who kept us on track and beat a continuous path to our door.

CHAPTER SEVEN

The Blessings Continue

As the week progressed, Larry felt better and better—in his words, "like nothing's wrong." He went to the Lions club and canvassed for a donation of $100 for the Good Samaritan Fund for nursing home residents, and kept busy all week.

On Friday, our family doctor notified us that we had an appointment with him on Monday at 11:00 a.m. We were not told why, just that we needed to be there. I arranged for Larry to pick me up at work so we could go together, and then I could return afterwards.

On Saturday, Larry got up early and sped to church to help with the men's breakfast. He cooked bacon and eggs for 55 men that morning and loved every minute of it. That afternoon our friends from Chicago arrived, and he had incredible energy. I thought he would be so worn out but he was having too good a time.

We looked at pictures of ourselves 25 years earlier and just roared (all except the one guy, Bill, who looked the same. He still looked just like Fonzie from *Happy Days*. Whoa!) Their visit was so well timed and it looked like Larry was on a high. We took pictures together and they all rubbed Larry's head for good luck before they left. That night Larry slept like a log. He was absolutely exhausted. Again I prayed,

Dianne Klancir

"Lord I have never asked once for a reason for any of this. I know there are reasons for everything and there is a greater good in everything that happens. I trust in You with my whole heart. I pray only for Your will, whatever that is. I thank You for giving my husband his strength and his spirit back. Our lives are in Your hands and we can do nothing without You. Please continue to bless us and keep all our friends safe. Give our daughter the faith and courage she needs to cope with this from so far away. She has been so wonderful with her dad, and I can't imagine how hard it is every time she leaves here. Keep her safe in her travels. I ask these things in Your Son's name. Amen."

God sometimes answers our prayers in marvelous ways but doesn't want us to become preoccupied with the miraculous. I was careful not to pray for miracles. I wanted to remain focused on the miracle worker, whether or not another miracle occurred. It was time to "walk by faith and not by sight" (2 Corinthians 5:7).

It was Sunday, March 11th, 2001. I talked Larry into taking a walk around our lot to see how Spring was unveiling itself. Along the south side of the house, crocuses were sticking their noses out of the ground. Buds were awakening on the red bud tree and it wouldn't be long until the tulips would be blooming. Oh, for a glimpse of new life to revive a tired soul!

We went to church, and it was the first time that Larry had taken his cap off in public. Everyone commented on how good he looked with his new hairstyle—or lack of it. (His head got so cold he wore a knitted skull cap around the house in the dreaded orange and navy colors. "Go Chicago Bears!" as my husband would say.)

We relaxed most of the day preparing for a busy Monday and a visit with our family physician. I was sure he just wanted to see Larry to keep abreast of what was happening with him. We were feeling so positive, nothing could drag us down. I've heard it said that when you

THE GIFT OF TODAY

are so confident, you don't fully understand your situation. I believe that confidence comes from faith, knowing that God is always there no matter what. It isn't always necessary to have all the answers and understand everything. God knows the answers and He understands the situation.

Monday came and Larry picked me up at work for his doctor visit. Our family doctor was a young fellow, but one that we had come to trust and respect. This was our first visit with him since Larry was diagnosed. He wanted us to go back to the beginning of what happened, find out what tests had been performed, and determine if we had questions about Larry's condition and chemo. The one concern I wanted to address while we were there was whether Larry had developed a urinary tract infection and needed an antibiotic. He confirmed that for us. Apparently, the chemo affected the immune system rapidly and he was more susceptible to things like that. The doctor had not received all the reports from the pulmonologist and oncologist yet, so there were many "holes in the total picture" for him. He did inform us that just because the oncologist gave us a time line, that it wasn't cast in concrete. He said that often people live much longer than the expected prognosis.

He was trying to be helpful. But it was the first time I had to relive everything and say it all out loud, and when we got in the car I absolutely lost it. I didn't want to cry in front of Larry but I couldn't help it. There he was comforting me, and I was the one who should have been comforting him. I told him how this seemed like a nightmare, and I kept thinking we would wake up and everything would be normal again. It was the first time since the day he was diagnosed that I had allowed him to see me in a less than positive light.

I was in awe of his courage through this. I wanted to continue with his treatments, have a positive outlook every day, and not let this get the better of us. If there was something we could find humor in, we got a laugh out of it. Anyway, we were not going to let one bad experience get us down for very long. We tried to focus on the positive, rather than the negative. It's all about choices.

The next day Pastor Mike came by for a visit. He was a very uplifting man; very dedicated to ministering to the sick. He was formerly a physician's assistant so he was well educated about medical conditions. His visits always had a very calming influence on us.

Larry decided that day to go bowling for the first time with his senior friends. Because it was an older group, the environment wasn't nearly as smoky as it was when some of the younger leagues were there. The seniors were always good for a few laughs, so I was relieved he felt well enough to join them. In the process of motivating himself to return to bowling, he also motivated his good friend Dave, whose impaired eyesight had kept him from bowling for many years. Dave decided that if Larry could bowl with everything he was going through, he could too. To this day, Dave still bowls and he truly enjoys it.

We received Larry's blood test results on Wednesday and PRAISE GOD, his red blood cell levels had all increased back to normal ranges. His white blood cells were still in normal range, so he was doing excellent! No transfusions for this man—just more apricots and raisins with a raw spinach salad thrown in for good measure!

Larry informed me that he asked his doctor to fax a return to work slip. The doctor agreed and said he could go back "as tolerated." He wanted to return on Thursday. I was so pleased. Larry had a wonderful supervisor who told him that if he needed an extra break or two throughout the day he should take it; if he was winded he should sit down, or if he needed to cut the day short, he should do so. What a blessing! Larry could have easily quit that job and stayed home. He was certainly of an age to do so, but he didn't want to sit around and think about his illness.

He made it through seven hours the first day back and came home TIRED. He decided to go back the next day though. I chose to let

THE GIFT OF TODAY

him make his own decisions and not interfere because at this point, he seemed to know what was best for him. God was looking out for him and I knew he would be alright.

That Friday evening, one of the adults with developmental disabilities, from my place of employment, was invited to spend the night at our house. She had been there for visits and overnights before, and we had made her a promise about a month earlier, that if she met all her goals at work, she could spend the night. I told Larry I would postpone her visit if he wanted me to, but he insisted she come over. He just loved her and so did I. She was in her 40's but it was like having a small child in the house. She was a lot of fun to have around and was always smiling, so I knew she would be good for Larry. She had become very fond of him because he was always so kind to her. We had not told her about his diagnosis. We just said he had a bad cold. Our friend arrived and she kept us on our toes. We made lasagna and garlic bread for supper, she took pictures with us, and we baked brownies and nine dozen cookies for church fellowship on Sunday. We lit candles and listened to piano music during dinner, and she said, "It's so peaceful at your house." That simple phrase was music to my ears. How wonderful that in the midst of our turmoil, we presented a peaceful existence to this precious lady.

Saturday morning when we awakened there was two inches of unexpected snow on the ground, and Larry couldn't wait to rev up the snow plow one more time. It was his favorite toy. We took our friend to lunch and shopping for some new clothes. It was a beautiful sunny day filled with the simplicities of life and a good friend.
Sunday was another sunny day in the low 60's with a gentle breeze, and at our house, after a long winter that meant PICNIC!!!

I remembered back to a specific day, many years ago, when we packed up a picnic lunch and headed to a wonderful park in Freeport, about 30 miles away. On the way, we had some dark clouds pass over and the wind picked up terribly. We were caught in the worst hail storm and tornado watch we had ever experienced. Larry had to pull over to the side of the road because the hail was so deep on the street, the car was sliding around. We sat there a good 10 minutes waiting for this to pass over and then continued on to the park. I remembered looking at Dina in the back seat and asking if she was okay. She gave us a rather sheepish smile and said, "I'm okay, but are we gonna have a picnic in this weather?"

By the time we got to the picnic ground, the sun was out in all its glory. We wiped all the hail off the table, spread out our tablecloth and cooked our hamburgers. We were the only ones out there.

On 80 and 90 degree days when everyone else was having picnics, we tended to do other things. However, let there be a sunny spring day after a long cold winter, and we were at the picnic grounds.

On this Spring Sunday, we went to Subway and got sandwiches and gravitated to a peaceful spot by the Oregon dam. We would listen to the rush of the water and let the sounds carry us away. We stayed out there the better part of the day. Once the sun started going down, Yul's (Larry's) head started getting cold and his knitted cap wasn't doing the job. It was time to call it a day.

On Monday, Larry was to return for his next chemo treatment. The appointment started out with a chest x-ray in order to compare the size of the tumor to the previous x-ray. The oncologist's jaw dropped. When she put the x-rays side by side, there was a huge difference, already, after one round of treatment.

She exclaimed, "This is incredible! Look at the difference here. What have you been doing?"

We told her we were praying and living our lives for that day only, knowing that God was in charge and Larry would be okay. She was so thrilled. "Well, just keep that up," she responded.

THE GIFT OF TODAY

The second treatment went very well. They were pre-medicating him with Decadron® (a steroid), Benadryl® (an antihistamine), Anzimet® (a very expensive anti-nausea drug) and Tagamet® (to protect his stomach and help digest his morning meal). It worked beautifully. There were no ill-effects from the chemo.

His next appointment was scheduled to be in early April, but we were planning to take a little vacation and the oncologist didn't want his blood levels dropping while we were gone, so it was postponed one week.

The next day Larry attended the Cancer Survivors Tea at the Country Club with his friend Earl. It was the first time Larry had been in a suit and tie since his new hairstyle. He looked so handsome. Ninety-five percent of the attendees were women, and the two of them were the center of attention. Larry admitted that he never took his cap off because he was a little self-conscious. *Yikes! Not exactly great etiquette at the Country Club, but when you have cancer you can get away with that.* He said it was a little cool in there and his head was cold. *I wondered if Michael Jordan had that problem.*

Larry returned from the tea with this food-for-thought: "Look to this day. Yesterday is always a dream and tomorrow is only a vision. But, today, well-lived, makes yesterday a dream of happiness, and every tomorrow a VISION OF HOPE. Amen." (anonymous)

We couldn't have agreed more.

CHAPTER EIGHT

Spring Brings the Promise of New Life

*L*arry made it through day three of chemo treatment with just a little discomfort in his joints and muscles. On that particular day, he also noted that foods that had formerly been his favorites, now tasted terrible. "Metallic" was the word he used.

Our daughter, Dina, was scheduled to arrive the next day and spend a few days with us. It was her Golden Birthday—23 years old on the 23rd of March. Dina's birthdays were always a celebration at our house. Larry and I believed that special moments should be celebrated— break out the good china, have a party, and do it up right.

I remembered all the way back to Dina's first birthday. Both sides of the family were invited and we used a nursery rhyme theme. A series of cakes were decorated to look like the three little pigs, a house of straw, a house of bricks and a house of wood. It was adorable. I had never taken a cake decorating class, but I did the best I could each year by copying a picture from a magazine. One year she had a Bert & Ernie cake and a Sesame Street theme; one year it was Holly Hobbie,

THE GIFT OF TODAY

and so on. When she reached school age, there were parties at the house with games and goodie bags. One year we took all the kids to a popular kid's restaurant for pizza. Another year we went to the roller rink and had a party. Each year it was something different and her day was always a special one that she remembered throughout the years.

When she turned 13, we rented the local pizza place for dinner, and then held a dance at our house afterwards. That was the year that we had just finished our basement and her party was the first event held down there. My husband had installed drywall, painted, laid new carpeting, put in a false ceiling, etc. It looked great until the kids started having ice cube fights and tore down the dark blue crepe paper that hung from the ceiling. Because it was wet, it stained the new carpet. Larry and I were not happy campers. Fortunately, it came out with a little elbow grease. The antics of 13-year olds!

This particular year, we had a formal dinner at home the evening before Dina's 23rd birthday. She opened gifts and we all watched the movie, *Remember the Titans*. Dina planned to spend her actual birthday with her dad. I went to work and they had the entire day together. They walked around the yard and looked at the new growth on the evergreen trees, the tulips blooming and the irises that were about to pop open. (Irises are Dina's favorite flowers.) They went bowling—Larry was still champ. They bought sandwiches and ate lunch at our favorite spot by the dam. Afterward, they dropped by my workplace. Returning home, they gravitated to the air hockey table in the family room for three intense games. Larry won two out of three, retaining his title of champ there also! He had a highly competitive spirit that couldn't be dampened by cancer or chemo treatments.

Larry and Dina talked a lot that day. Dina gave her dad a journal and asked him to write down his thoughts each day. I thought that was a marvelous idea. Larry was a man of few words, and sometimes we weren't quite sure what he was feeling. It was equally hard for him to write things down because he was self-conscious about his grammar. Dina promised that if he wrote down his thoughts and sent them to her, she would reply by writing her thoughts in the journal and returning it. That was all he needed to hear. It created a very special bond between them. I never asked what was written in that journal. It was very personal between the two of them.

That evening we joined Dina, her boyfriend Matt, and 15 of her friends at a favorite pizza place to celebrate her birthday.

We couldn't believe that she wanted us along at this party, but her friends always thought that Larry and I were "cool," as they put it. Not because we were the kind of parents that allowed drinking and making-out at parties when she was growing up. In fact, it was quite the opposite. We were the parents who set boundaries. Behaviors at our parties had to be "age appropriate".

The place where we met had a large bar at one end of the room. I was afraid it might get quite smoky in there so the waiter seated us as far from the bar as possible. Dina's friends greeted us very warmly and made Larry feel extra special.

It had been over three years since we'd seen some of her friends and they now seemed so mature. We'd known some of the kids since they were five years old and they had grown into wonderful adults. Some were engaged, some married, and some had traveled extensively. It was a great time. We left Dina and her friends at 9:00 p.m., delighted to have been included and pleased to see how they rallied around and supported her. They partied until 2:00 a.m. Dina proclaimed it her best birthday ever.

After lunch the next day, Dina and Matt headed back to Madison. Larry and I watched the movie, *Meet the Parents,* and I never saw him laugh so hard. He felt every guy who had a daughter should see that movie.

Later, Larry received a call from a member of our church, Warren,

THE GIFT OF TODAY

inviting him to the upcoming Father-Son Banquet. The funny part was that this man was younger than my husband and wanted Larry to go as his son! Neither had anyone to accompany them to the banquet, so they laughingly decided to go together. It was so thoughtful of Warren to think of Larry and give him another opportunity to be out among friends. We also got the word that Larry's golf cart was tuned up and ready to go. He would be ready for opening day at the course in April. Hallelujah!

Larry continued to work about four days a week and his condition remained stable. Recent blood work showed that his hemoglobin had dropped to 11.9, but was still well within acceptable range. Platelets had also dropped to 219. His white count was holding however. So back we went on the high iron diet of kidney beans, lentils, leafy dark greens, and—you know the rest—raisins, apricots and liver.

Things were going along nicely. We looked forward to an upcoming family vacation in Branson, Missouri, to celebrate my parent's 50th wedding anniversary. Dina called to tell us she was promoted to case manager, with a nice pay increase. Another prayer had been answered. We felt like we were being given a rest period and it was a very welcome rest. At that particular time, a dear friend had e-mailed us the following:

The Music of Your Life
There is no music during a musical rest, but the rest is part of the making of the music. In the melody of our life, the music is separated here and there by rests. During those rests, we foolishly believe we have come to the end of the song. God sends us times of forced leisure by allowing sickness, disappointed plans and frustrated efforts. He brings a sudden pause in the choral hymn of our lives, and we lament that our voices must be silent. We grieve that our part is missing in the music that continually rises to the ear of our Creator. Yet how

does a musician read the rest? He counts the break with wavering precision and plays his next note with confidence, as if no pause were ever there.

God does not write the music of our lives without a plan. Our part is to learn the tune and not be discouraged during the rests. They are not to be slurred over or omitted, nor used to destroy the melody or to change the key. If we will only look up, God Himself will count the time for us. With our eyes on Him, our next note will be full and clear. If we sorrowfully say to ourselves, "There is no music in a rest," let us not forget that the rest is part of the making of the music. The process is often slow and painful in this life, yet how patiently God works to teach us! And how long He waits for us to learn the lesson! (By John Ruskin).

It was such an appropriate item to send to us at that time. We were trying to think of this period as a "rest" in God's music for our lives.

As the days went on, I continued to be amazed. I saw my husband laugh out loud at things he would have never considered funny before. He was enjoying life to its fullest. There were no complaints about his physical health and he was looking forward to opening day of golf, which was now only 36 hours away (*but who's counting???*).

Because golf was one of the things I always considered a competitor for my husband's attention, when he asked me to join him on the course on Sunday, I could not refuse. He had to exhibit extreme patience, but the important thing was that we were out there together doing something he loved and we were getting some exercise. We had a great time together and I actually added my name to Larry's membership at the course.

That evening my dear friend Kris called to inform me that we needed a "girl's night out." I hadn't spent an evening away from my

THE GIFT OF TODAY

husband in an awfully long time and felt guilty about leaving him alone. But he agreed that Kris and I needed to spend time together.

She and I had always been able to tell each other just about anything without fearing that it would affect our friendship. Kris had also been through a lot. Her mother had passed away around Christmas, after a long respiratory illness. She needed to talk about her ordeal too.

We sat in the restaurant talking, laughing and crying for three hours. Kris, with her cheeseburger and onion peels, me, with a cup of coffee and low-fat brownie sundae. It was the safe environment we both needed to release emotions that had been held inside too long. Seeing the need for privacy, our waitress eventually told us to take all the time we needed, and signal her if we wanted something. She even brought a box of tissues. People probably thought we were crazy but we didn't care. It was so cleansing. I didn't realize how much I needed that "girl time."

The next week Larry developed laryngitis again and I became concerned. The first bout of laryngitis had quickly disappeared after his first chemo treatment. According to the oncologist, that was because the tumor had been pressed against the nerves that controlled his voice box. Chemo had reduced the tumor and released the pressure. With the laryngitis back, the oncologist wanted more blood work.

We were one week away from a vacation that I wasn't sure we should take. His white blood cell count had dropped significantly (to 3.4), which meant he was unable to fight off infection now. She started him on Neupogen® shots that same day, which stimulate the bone marrow to produce white blood cells. He was to receive an injection every day that week. On Friday they would repeat the blood work before we left for our trip.

The oncologist warned that he would have some aches and pains in his long bones, and most likely in his breastbone. That meant that the bone marrow was doing its thing as his system competed to replenish white blood cells. It was all so complicated, but we learned in a hurry.

The injections were very expensive. In order for our insurance to pay, we had to drive 80 miles round trip to a designated hospital in Rockford. If that was the worst thing we had to do, we would certainly live with that. Larry reported pain after the first injection but it was relieved by Tylenol®.

He worked five-hour days for four days that week, and played nine holes of golf at least three days. He also drove me to and from work each day, and insisted on driving the 80-mile round trip for his injections. Pretty impressive. When Larry was first diagnosed with stage IV cancer, my immediate reaction was "rest and don't overdo." Then I realized that the best thing for him was to continue to do that which he loved. Rest means different things to different people. I came across this article that described that difference very well.

"Two painters were once asked to paint a picture illustrating their own ideas of rest. The first chose for his scene a quiet, lonely lake, nestled among mountains far away. The second, using swift, broad strokes on his canvas, painted a thundering waterfall. Beneath the falls grew a fragile birch tree, bending over the foam. On its branches, nearly wet with the spray from the falls, sat a robin on its nest. The first painting was simply a picture of stagnation and inactivity. The second, however, depicted rest." (Anonymous)

I was so grateful that Larry had not chosen stagnation, but rather a level of activity that he found restful, yet satisfying.

I shopped for our trip that week, still very hopeful that we were going on vacation. While shopping, I purchased two magnetic earrings for him. One was an anchor and the other was a peace sign. Dina and I thought that with this new bald look he should have an earring, and there was no way we were going to pierce his ears with his blood

THE GIFT OF TODAY

counts as they were. He laughed so hard when I brought them home, but he did wear them. They allowed him to express himself and he got tons of compliments. We had to find humor in all of this somehow.

Larry continued to feel a tickling sensation in his throat that made him cough. He still had some laryngitis after his third shot, and he complained of pain in his upper arms and legs on the third day. He stayed off the golf course and said it felt like a bad case of flu.

When I told the doctor, she postponed the last two shots and had him come in for blood work on Friday. The oncologist said that if his white count was over 10.0 he could discontinue the shots. The doctor was shocked that his counts had soared to 21.1!

"STOP THOSE SHOTS!" she ordered. "If you were in front of me right now, I'd hug you!"

She did caution us that the white blood cell count would drop almost 50% by the following day. The injections had tricked the bone marrow into thinking that it didn't have to work so hard, but that would quickly level off.

Larry was feeling better, looked great and my only concern was that he was still hoarse. The good news was that the oncologist felt we could go on vacation without worrying.

We were gratefully relieved. Our prayer was this:

"Lord, help us not to focus on what may happen tomorrow, but rather to live in the present and be grateful for those blessings which You have bestowed upon us. The same God who cares for us today will continue to take care of us. He will protect us from suffering or will give us His strength that we may endure it. Grant us peace, and help us forget all our anxious thoughts and worries. All Glory to God! I pray in Jesus' name. Amen."

We packed our bags and took the dog to the kennel. Sunday we drove to Edwardsville, Illinois, without incident and arrived in Branson, Missouri on Monday. We were joining my parents and two

Dianne Klancir

of my three sisters and their families for this celebration. I warned the family ahead of time via e-mail that Larry would look different, so that everyone wouldn't be shocked. He had aged some, lost weight and was bald—with an earring, yet!

Dina couldn't vacation with us, but she and Matt would join us Easter weekend when we returned. They had gotten a puppy, Delia, in Alaska where they both worked the previous summer, and she would accompany them to our house. Delia was part Labrador, part Rotweiller. We weren't sure how our own Bichon-Cocker, Molly, would accept Delia but we'd make it work. It would be a lively Easter!

We couldn't have asked for more at this time. Larry had come through each treatment with grace and strength that surpassed our wildest dreams. When the cancer diagnosis invaded our lives, we learned to live the way God intended—taking each day and each moment for what it was worth and enjoying it to the fullest. We learned to leave the rest to God.

"God is in every tomorrow,
therefore I live for today.
Certain of finding at sunrise,
guidance and strength for my way;
Power for each moment of weakness,
hope for each moment of pain,
Comfort for every sorrow,
sunshine and joy after rain. Amen." (By Al Bryant)

CHAPTER NINE

Vacation At Last

We were actually leaving on a trip. It was just too good to be true. The drive went very well, although Larry became tired and I drove more than normal. I was glad he was willing to turn that over to me.

I hadn't seen my family since Thanksgiving when we had celebrated an early Christmas together. Now, five months later, eleven of us would gather for my parents' 50th anniversary. Only my sister Margie and her family could not attend.

My parents had a time-share that allowed them beautiful condo vacations in Branson, Missouri, and were able to book individual condos for each family with their "points." Bobbie, the youngest, and her family of five, drove down from northern Minnesota. Cathy, six years younger than me, drove from Oshkosh, Wisconsin, with her husband Michael. Larry and I were driving from northern Illinois. It all worked out so well. We had beautiful places to stay and would all be together.

Everyone was delighted to see Larry and there was laughter as well as tears. Naturally, everyone commented on his hip new look with an earring and shaved head. I teased him that if we each got tattoos, black leathers and a Harley®, we could go on the road. He wasn't buying it. Besides, he was a Honda® guy at heart.

Anyway, after checking into our units, we met at my parent's condo. They had planned a "mystery dinner" for all of us. *Leave it to them.* We were each given a menu and had to order our dinner using the clues given. There were 17 items and we were to order 16—some were food, some were utensils. *Interesting.* There were four courses to the meal and four items for each course.

We didn't actually know what to expect until it was placed in front of us. Cathy and I were served the pudding dessert first, with a beverage, a napkin and knife. For the next course, Bobbie and I got corn and jello with no silverware at all. (The knife was removed after the first course). Now think about eating those two items without silverware! Larry managed to receive his dinner in just the right order with the correct utensils to boot. I think it was rigged!

That silly dinner was just the beginning of a great week together. It was so good to be surrounded by family—laughing, recalling family events, and playing games with my ten and twelve-year old nieces and four-year old nephew.

During the day we usually shopped, went sightseeing, or to a movie or show together. (Although one rainy morning we decided to relax and be leisurely. It felt good to stop and smell the roses.)

There was even time for miniature golf. Needless to say, Larry won. Although I did have two holes-in-one, it was just never enough to beat him.

One evening we gathered at my parent's condo for the "official" 50th anniversary party. We presented them with the quilted wall-hanging featuring fabric photos of all their children and families. That was the photo we'd taken when Larry had just been diagnosed. It turned out great, but it was the first time Larry had seen a recent picture of himself, and he couldn't believe how he'd changed. Like I said, it wasn't the picture I wanted hanging in my parent's living

THE GIFT OF TODAY

room forever. But, it's who we were at the time and we just had to live with that.

The condo community hosted dinner and entertainment one night, with Larry and me as part of the entertainment! We were one of five couples chosen to play the *Not-So-Newlywed Game*. We were TERRIBLE! But we laughed so hard. Some of the questions were very personal and some were just plain ridiculous, but it was all in good fun.

Later that evening we saw the Jim Stafford show, which included not only his musical entertainment and humor, but a terrific laser light show. It was a great way to end the day.

The morning we all departed, the whole family went to a breakfast show featuring comedian, Yakov Smirnoff. It was two hours of solid laughter. Our sides actually hurt when we left! Following the show, we all said goodbye and headed for home. It was sad to see everyone go their separate ways knowing we wouldn't see each other again for several months, but we were so grateful for the opportunity to be together.

I drove to St. Louis, Missouri, where we spent the night. Larry slept almost the entire time in the car. Then, he bundled himself in a blanket when we reached the hotel and slept until I woke him for dinner. He was so drained. After dinner, he went to bed and slept until morning without waking.

The next day he insisted he was alert enough to drive. I could soon tell that the stress of driving was getting to him. He made a couple of poor decisions behind the wheel that almost hurt us and another vehicle full of people. When I begged him to pull over and let me drive he became very defensive and stubborn. *Why was it suddenly*

Dianne Klancir

so important to be in control? Just a week ago he had let me share the driving. Fortunately, with many prayers offered up, we made it home safely.

Dina planned to spend Easter with us and was waiting when we returned Friday afternoon. She had picked up the dog at the kennel, bathed her, cleaned the bathrooms, baked a cake and washed her car. No grass growing under those feet! We all attended the Good Friday church service and shared a nice dinner together.

Saturday morning started at 6 a.m. when Larry rose early to make steak, eggs and hash browns for 61 men at the Christian men's breakfast. When he got back I dropped him at the golf course while I did some fundraising for an annual auction. He played 16 holes and did remarkably well. Dina's boyfriend, Matt, arrived that afternoon and they took off to party with friends after dinner.

Easter Sunday we all went to church together, which was a wonderful treat for Larry and me. Afterward, Larry grilled corn on the cob and we had rock cornish hens with wild rice dressing. Everyone ate until they were stuffed.

As soon as Larry and Matt could escape, they headed for the golf course. Dina stayed behind to play softball catch with me. It gave us a chance to visit and it brought back fond memories of Dina, Larry and me playing catch in the backyard. We spent many evenings doing that. Sometimes Larry and Dina went out and he would work with her on pitching. She got upset occasionally, feeling that he was overly critical, but he was trying to teach her. Yes, they did have their moments. But for the most part, it was always good quality time together.

I had always loved softball and played either shortstop or first base. Dina was a natural shortstop and a pretty decent pitcher. She was not

THE GIFT OF TODAY

afraid of the ball, that's for sure. And, she had a throw that could burn a hole through a mitt.

The kids left for Madison about 5:00 p.m. that Easter Sunday and we got the call two hours later that they had arrived home safely. It was a fine week.

Monday morning we were to return to the oncologist. She had called on Friday for an update on Larry's condition. When I told her that he still had laryngitis and became confused a couple of times behind the wheel, she immediately scheduled a CAT scan of his brain. If the CAT scan came back clean, he could have his chemo treatment. If not, we would move to radiation of the brain.

I remembered a prayer from Archbishop Leighton that described how we felt:

"*When God is the center of a soul, although disasters may crowd in on all sides and roar like the waves of the sea, there is a constant calm within. The world can neither give nor take away that kind of peace.*"

We were feeling God's peace and it would sustain us through all our personal struggles.

CHAPTER TEN

Back to the Routine

Monday morning we were to be in Rockford at 8:30 a.m. for Larry's CT of the brain. Due to the personality changes I experienced on this trip, I asked the oncologist not to leave any stone unturned. She ordered the scan "STAT" (as soon as possible) so that if there was a tumor or cancer cells, he could begin radiation immediately. The CT came back clean and his blood levels were within normal limits. *Praise God!* The doctor felt that the stress of the trip, and driving in an unfamiliar place with a lack of self-confidence, caused the confusion.

Future trips would be handled differently, as we couldn't afford to have any more close calls like the one we had. It was a very scary feeling for me, so I tried to imagine what it was like for Larry.

He was scheduled for a chest x-ray also, and struck a pose for the "camera." The x-ray showed that the tumor was still resting against the bronchus and nerves controlling his voice box—thus, the laryngitis. There was just a very slight difference in the size of the tumor this time. The biggest difference was that there was considerably less fluid in his left lung. He was back to almost total function in the left lung, and the flow of oxygen was excellent!

Larry developed a slight headache and stomachache during the

THE GIFT OF TODAY

chemotherapy treatment later that day and decided to take Pepcid AC® twice a day for stomach discomfort. Tylenol® was controlling the headaches. I asked for something stronger for his pain and the oncologist was very willing to give him whatever he needed. She wrote a prescription for Vicodin®, which he decided not to take yet.

The oncologist told us again how proud she was of Larry's progress and his courage, and the way we worked as a team.

"I wish every patient that came in had the spousal support that you do," she marveled. "It's obvious that you're fighting this disease together."

Larry continued to have that nagging stomach discomfort for a few days and food didn't appeal to him much.

On day three of chemo that week, Larry was flat out wasted. He was unable to go to work for a half-day, and unable to golf. His arms and legs were killing him, and he had his first wave of nausea when I put supper in front of him. He asked me to go to the store and buy canned soups and ice cream. (I chose other things to buy for him as ice cream, in particular, is not something to put in front of someone who is nauseated). He didn't want me going to the trouble of cooking for him and have the smell of food make him sick. I loved to cook, so it didn't bother me, but I knew it bothered him.

He tried taking his golf cart out that evening on the course and I went with him. By the 6th hole, he could barely swing the club. We came home and I knew he was feeling a little defeated. I didn't want to discourage him from going out because he seemed to know what he could handle. But; he was starting to realize how these treatments would affect him and that he would have to slow down for a while.

He still refused the Vicodin® so I gave him three extra-strength Tylenol® and a good backrub before he fell asleep.

Dianne Klancir

I prayed that evening from Psalm 32:
"If I see God in everything, He will calm and color everything I see. Perhaps the circumstances causing my sorrows will not be removed and my situation will remain the same, but if Christ is brought into my grief and gloom as my Lord and Master, He will surround me with songs of deliverance."

The following day, he ached all over. He couldn't go to work. He couldn't golf or bowl. He had a restless night, and I pressed him to take a Vicodin® but he didn't want to give in to that yet. He wanted to continue with Tylenol® for as long as possible. I tried to explain about staying ahead of the pain, but he was worried about getting addicted to painkillers. I wanted him to have relief so he could sleep.

At some point, if he wasn't going to switch to a stronger painkiller, I knew that I would have to step in and decide for him. I wasn't trying to take away his independence or his rights, but sometimes in these situations people don't make clear judgments and others need to take charge.

I cannot stress enough how important advocacy is for a patient. It's important that someone asks physicians to explain procedures and test results that the patient doesn't understand, but may hesitate to question. It's important that someone asks the necessary questions and requests the pain relievers that the patient needs, if it isn't readily offered. I believed in my heart that everyone we had encountered up to that point was doing their level best to keep us informed, to listen to us and empower us with the knowledge we needed to fight this disease. Not everyone who has had experience with the medical profession can say that.

The following day Larry still ached all over. He was up every hour during the night, which meant I was also up. We both felt a little sleep

THE GIFT OF TODAY

deprived after two consecutive restless nights. And yet, he refused the Vicodin®. My patience was wearing thin.

He was eating only canned soup, canned puddings and jello. Occasionally I would get him to drink a Sprite® or 7-Up®. And, once in awhile he would accept a protein drink that provided extra calories, but that wasn't every day.

The laryngitis was so bad that his voice was mostly forced air, and at times he was difficult to understand. I told him it was because he was so full of hot air! He just shook his head and smiled. I gave him a pad of paper and a pencil and asked him to conserve his voice and write down what he had to say just like we had done in the hospital. That helped relieve his exhaustion and frustration somewhat.

I was forced to admit that this dreaded chemo does get worse as treatments progress. True, he was in good spirits and had only lost eight pounds since the diagnosis. But food had lost its appeal, he was tired, and was having pain in his extremities.

I decided that evening that we needed to do something different. I got out some old videos of our daughter's basketball games when she began playing in 5th grade. It was great medicine. We watched those videos and laughed until we had tears in our eyes. The girls looked so awkward and clumsy when they were first learning and they would bunch up in this little group and hand each other the ball. There was screaming and yelling and very little actual basketball was played. With each year, naturally, the girls got better. Finally, we got to the 8th grade level of play and could see dramatic improvement. There was actual passing and dribbling (without traveling) and some pretty impressive shooting. It was amazing to see how they developed. It was so much fun to watch them grow and learn, not only about the game, but about life. They learned patience, how to work as a team, and that sometimes you'll get knocked down and you have to get right back up.

Dianne Klancir

Larry and I held hands while we watched the videos. Sometimes we laughed and sometimes our eyes filled with tears. But, we were always impressed by this great group of girls.

Strangely, one of the games my husband taped disappeared after we watched it that evening. It was the game when Larry lost his temper with the referees. He wasn't always a good sport at some of those games, due mainly to his very competitive nature. There were a few times I had actually threatened to leave events without him if I saw a questionable call and knew he would be upset about it. Love is blind, and he had a tendency to think that his daughter (and her teammates) never made a mistake on the basketball or volleyball court, the baseball diamond or the track. Most of the time, I was able to keep his comments to a minimum, but that particular night he and I were separated at the game, and when I heard the yelling coming from his direction of the gym, I ran! He had set the video camera down but had not turned it off. His inappropriate behavior came through loud and clear! He was so embarrassed when he heard it played back that I never saw that tape again.

The next couple days were pretty uneventful, and we seemed to be in a "resting" stage again. We were able to live a pretty normal life—if that's possible with cancer—and even went golfing together.

It was only the second or third time in 20 years I had been on the course, and I'm not sure who laughed more, Larry or me. My score was 83 for nine holes! Let me tell you, I was exhausted. It wasn't easy to golf that badly! I swung more times in nine holes than Larry did in 18.

"Are you sure you don't mind playing this game?" he asked. "I mean, you're not very good at it."

"Thank you dear," I replied patiently. "But I can enjoy something without having to be good at it. And thank God for that, or there isn't much in this world I would enjoy."

THE GIFT OF TODAY

I saw a spark in him again and on our way home he asked, "Would you mind making me some creamed asparagus on toast tonight?"

Well, I was not only pleased, I was ecstatic!

He had gotten his appetite back but still couldn't taste everything. Some things still seemed to have a peculiar flavor. And he was getting very tired of soup, pudding and Jello®.

That evening, after golf, I decided to make a loaf of homemade bread with the accelerated speed of our breadmaker while preparing the fresh asparagus. Larry napped and eventually woke up to the smell of fresh bread baking. He adored that smell. I placed the food in front of him piping hot, and he took in the aroma. He looked up at me and smiled. "Thank you, Dee, I love you."

"It's my pleasure honey, and I love you too,"

He dug into that food and after several bites, turned to me and asked, "Is it good?"

"You would love it." I answered. He just kept on eating with a huge grin on his face. *Our conversations were definitely getting stranger.*

Within the next couple days, we would both return to work and he would get his taste buds back. The man's appetite was ravenous and I couldn't make enough to fill him up. In two days he ate four stuffed peppers for lunch, six lemon poppyseed muffins disappeared, and he requested brownies—twice! And he didn't even appreciate chocolate!

The evening after we golfed, three members of the local theater group, the Performing Arts Guild (PAG), paid Larry a surprise visit. Larry and his buddy Dick had become active in PAG the past few years building sets for plays. They had gotten quite innovative with the materials they had to work with at times.

Larry was not the kind of guy who wanted to be on stage. He would rather work silently behind the scenes constructing something.

However, I have to say that their work was anything but silent, because most of the time they were hammering away and laughing about something. Dick was also a co-worker in the Maintenance Department at the nursing home where Larry worked. He and Larry worked so well together on everything they did. Dick was one of the reasons Larry enjoyed his job so much.

That evening, Dick and two other PAG members presented him with a framed poster from the last play he had worked on, *Guys and Dolls*. It was signed by the entire cast, wishing Larry well and thanking him for all his hard work. He was extremely touched by that. Larry was never the kind of guy who looked for any glory and it was so heartwarming to know that his efforts were appreciated. That simple gesture did so much to boost his spirits.

That evening I prayed as I watched Larry sleep peacefully.

"Lord, I humbly focus my heart on You. I thank You for this day and for the fact that my husband rests tonight after being able to enjoy food for the first time in several days. Thank you for the beautiful day You provided for us – some spring rain followed by a warm sunny day that we could enjoy together on the golf course. Thank you for keeping me strong physically and mentally so that I may be a caregiver for my husband. Thank you for keeping us safe from danger and for blessing us repeatedly. I ask that You continue to assist us in seeing all this through God's eyes. And I ask that You not allow me to whine or whimper. Help me to remember that when I feel the world closing in, I should find a quiet place to retreat and just say Your name. I know that You know what is in my heart and that I truly love this man. I ask that You continue to uplift us that we may be an inspiration to others. And I pray for those who do not know You intimately and think they have to deal with the world's problems alone. I pray that I will never forget there is no situation greater than You. This is my prayer, in Jesus' name. Amen."

CHAPTER ELEVEN

Finding Humor in Everything

When things went well, they went REALLY well. It was a time when Larry felt so good. We were able to find humor in every situation that came up. Sometimes we just looked at each other and laughed for no reason. It was the most incredibly wonderful feeling.

There were other times that we laughed at something, and then as hard as we were laughing, I would start crying. Larry would look at me in disbelief and ask what had happened. It felt so good to laugh and release that emotion that I also released the tears that I worked so hard to hold inside. At first, I think I felt guilty finding something humorous with everything that was going on in our lives. But I believed then—and still do—that humor plays a huge role in a patient's recovery. We tried to find a way to laugh whenever we could.

I remembered a day we went shopping and out for dinner in Rockford. When we arrived home, there was a cylindrical cardboard container on our front porch about three inches in diameter and about 15 inches tall. It was labeled, "Your thank you gift from the Arbor Day Foundation." Larry asked if I knew what that was all about. I told him that about a month before I had sent them a donation and they were to send me ten trees in return. Larry looked at me and then at the container.

"I would like to think there is something else in here, or you had better start sending larger donations." he said. When we opened it, there were ten of the tiniest, dried-out branches with roots I had ever seen. All ten of them together were about as big around as a cigar and about five inches tall.

Larry held them up with two fingers and said, "And what should we do with these monsters?"

I was laughing so hard I could barely speak. I told him we would plant them around the perimeter of the yard and someday have a nice privacy fence. "I SHOULD LIVE SO LONG!" was his response.

The next thing I knew, he was in the yard with his cordless drill, drilling holes into the ground and sticking these twigs into them. The neighbors who were watching from their patio came over to ask what in the world he was doing.

"Oh, I'm planting a privacy fence for my wife."

The neighbors were practically rolling on the ground. I told them what had happened. They asked why we didn't just throw them out.

"Because they are trees and in 25 years we will have something that will cast a shadow. In the meantime, we just have to hope no one steps on them," he said cynically.

We just kept staring at them and laughing. They weren't even healthy looking five-inch tall twigs.

"For the next umpteen years," Larry added, "I have the joy of mowing around these babies, and God forbid if I would run one over. There would go the privacy fence."

We were literally holding each other up, we were laughing so hard.

I remembered when we went to Madison, Wisconsin, to spend the day with Dina. We started the day at the Farmer's Market and then took Molly and (Dina's dog) Delia to the dog park.

Those dogs played and ran until they literally dropped to the ground. Larry and I were people and dog watching, and began to

THE GIFT OF TODAY

laugh at the incredible resemblance we sometimes saw between dogs and their owners. One lady with a slight build, kinky black hair and little beady eyes, had a black poodle. There was a very slim man who had the longest legs I had ever seen. He was jogging with a Great Dane. And then there were some owners who looked like they were with the wrong dog. There was a lady that must have weighed over 300 pounds with a Chihuahua. That looked ridiculous. Larry turned to me and said, "That little dog had better hope he never winds up on the couch when she's ready to sit down. It would be 'goodbye doggie'." I couldn't believe he said that. We just roared.

In the midst of this 'good spell,' Larry's blood test revealed that his platelets and red blood cells were down slightly again. So we loaded up on fresh spinach salad with strawberries, marinated chicken breasts and Italian flatbread. Larry ate three bowls of spinach salad. As I was clearing away the plates, I asked if he needed any more. When he broke out into *The Popeye* theme song, I rolled my eyes and responded, "Okay, you're done," and just walked away laughing.

The following weekend we drove to Chicago for a very formal wedding. I was excited about this wedding because it was a very classy affair. I needed a new dress, so Larry helped me pick it out. He called it my "whoopee dress." Well, just the connotation of that phrase sent us both into laughter. It was champagne in color with a crocheted jacket, and there was long fringe from the sleeves and hem. It was a fun dress to wear!

We had the best time and our friends were thrilled to see us there; dressed up, dancing and enjoying ourselves so much. Larry and I walked from the parking lot to the church, and then to the reception that was a couple blocks away. We danced the evening away, and then had to walk back to the car. By the time we got there my feet were throbbing, but I didn't want to complain. Larry was in a great mood and sang in the car on the drive home.

The next morning, my feet were so swollen I couldn't even put on a pair of shoes, let alone walk. We both just stared at my feet and cracked up. I probably should have been crying, because my feet ached so badly they were screaming. Larry looked at them and said, "Those feet look like they belong on that lady with the Chihuahua at the dog park." Envisioning that picture from the day before, sent us both into laughter again.

The following day Larry was scheduled for chemotherapy. But when the doctor looked at his chest x-ray, she decided that the tumor was no longer shrinking. The fluid level in his lungs was low, but there was no change in the tumor size. So she wanted him to take a week off until she determined what the next step would be. I thought he would be upset. Instead, he grabbed my hand, waved goodbye to the oncologist, and said to me, "C'mon woman, I have a week of freedom. Let's party." He had everyone on that unit smiling.

When we got to the hallway, I said excitedly, "Let's hop in the elevator, jam up the buttons, have wild sex, run through the lobby naked and moon people all the way home."

"I can get in the elevator, jam up the buttons, run through the lobby naked and moon people," he replied. "But if you want wild sex, you had better hope there's another guy in there when the door opens." Again, hysterical laughter. When we got into the elevator, we hugged and kissed passionately. I loved this man, and he loved me.

It was the evening before Mother's day and we were expecting Dina to come home. We had planned a picnic for the following day. Larry said he felt that I needed to make a public apology to the congregation at church that our plans for a family picnic probably ruined what would have otherwise been a perfect weather day.

The weather report predicted a beautiful day, but we all knew that when our family planned a picnic, the weather would be anything but beautiful. We decided that rather than go to the picnic grounds, we

THE GIFT OF TODAY

would cook out in our backyard. It was a picture perfect afternoon—totally uncharacteristic of our family's usual outdoor events. We went for a long walk and played board games. We laughed a lot while reminiscing and it was so good for all of us.

Later, we watched a video of Dina playing her trumpet in a trio during a high school band competition.

The three trumpeters were playing in perfect harmony and everything was going along beautifully. Suddenly, as Dina began a solo, one of the valves on her trumpet stuck. She literally had to keep lifting the valve to continue playing. And, she did exactly that. She just continued on, struggling to stay with the music. When she played with the other two trumpets, everything was fine. But then she would solo again and the same thing happened. She never missed a beat. Larry and I were shocked, wondering if we should laugh or cry. We kept whispering to each other, "What is happening?"

After the performance, we consoled her and the other two players who had worked so hard on this piece. We were afraid their score would suffer and Dina would feel responsible. But the judges gave them a "1st" rating, which was the best possible, because she didn't give up, even with the faulty valve. Aside from that, their performance was perfect! We were very happy for them, but the sounds coming out of that trumpet had been horrible. One of the judges told her after the performance that he thought she had invented some new notes! It was a lot easier to laugh at the video than it was at the original performance.

The day after Mother's Day we were to get the new "recipe" for Larry's chemo and radiation program. My prayer was this:

"Lord, thank you for this beautiful day that I spent with my family. Thank you for the irises that bloomed in my flowerbed today, just in time for my daughter and I to enjoy. What a great Mother's Day gift! Thank you for a thoughtful and caring daughter. Thank you for the

103

Dianne Klancir

CAT scan results that showed my husband's tumor has not gotten any larger and that he has no new "spots." Thank you for helping my husband through this storm and finding his sense of humor again. Thank you for smiles, laughter and hope. May we never give up hope! I ask only for forgiveness for my many sins and that You continue to grant me patience for whatever lies ahead. I ask this in your Son's holy name. Amen."

On Monday we received the telephone call we'd been waiting for. His new "recipe" was ready and he should report for chemotherapy on Wednesday.

We discovered on Wednesday, that this new treatment (Carbogemzar®) only took two hours to run through the I.V. compared to at least five hours with the previous drug, Taxol®.

Following the chemo treatment, he reported to the radiation oncologist. (Another female, but this one much younger than his oncologist. Some of these doctors looked like kids.) They discussed his radiation treatments, a total of 30. They would be done daily, Monday through Friday. Then, he went through a simulation of his radiation treatment where they marked the site on his body where the treatment would focus.

Radiation treatments only lasted about two and one half MINUTES compared to the two-hour chemotherapy treatments. So, I only accompanied him on days when he had both chemo and radiation, or when the radiation treatment included a doctor visit. Whenever he had a "radiation only" visit, one of our friends would volunteer to accompany him. Afterward they would have lunch together, or go bowling or out for coffee. It gave me the opportunity to work and not spend forty-five minutes driving each way for a two-and-a-half minute treatment.

He handled the radiation beautifully. "Piece of cake," he said. And he was equally enthusiastic about the new chemo treatment.

THE GIFT OF TODAY

"It feels like an elephant has been lifted off my chest," he exclaimed after the first day. "Like something is chewing away at the tumors."
That put him in great spirits, of course. And, we heard the improvement in his voice quality almost immediately.

· The evening after his first new chemo treatment we managed to sneak in six holes at the golf course before it got so dark we couldn't see anymore. We rented the movie *Miss Congeniality*, which was great medicine. Larry adored Sandra Bullock and loved her performance in that film. He laughed so hard that tears streamed down his face. I wondered if she would be touched to know how entertaining her performance was to a cancer patient who needed to laugh.

After a few days of radiation, I noticed that Larry was more short of breath after exertion, although his color was better. He seemed to tire more easily and that wasn't what I expected with the radiation treatments. *Silly me.*

My parents arrived Saturday May 19th, my mother's birthday, and we celebrated that evening. On Sunday we were invited to my niece's high school graduation. We missed the ceremony but attended the party afterward. Larry needed a nap so we decided to catch up with everyone at the party.
Upon awakening, he complained of a little shoulder discomfort. Immediately, he feared that the cancer had spread to his bones. I reassured him that a bone scan had just been done and it was clean. I teased him instead that it was from all the golfing, and from his insatiable need to try to outplay me! Needless to say, he found that rather humorous.

My folks remained for the week to offer help and support. They accompanied Larry to his radiation treatments and kept him company one evening so I could go out with girlfriends.

The girls and I golfed on our evening out and I played the worst I ever had. But, it was so much fun! Sometimes I was laughing so hard that I could barely swing. *Good excuse, huh?* We went out for pizza afterwards. It was great respite for me.

I was grateful to my parents for being there and giving me a break that I hadn't realized I needed so much. I went along, day by day, trying to survive and keep up with the demands that were placed upon me. I just hadn't realized—or allowed myself to think about—how exhausting that was until I was removed from the situation.

When I got home that evening, Larry had a surprise for me. He had installed motion detector lights in the back of the house. We had bought those over a year ago and never gotten around to putting them up. I wasn't sure what possessed him to take on that project that particular evening (except that my dad, a retired electrician, was there to help him), but I certainly appreciated it. He informed me that my "boyfriend would no longer be able to lurk around the house now without being spotted." *Yeah, right.*

The following week Larry's chemo treatment was changed from Carbogemzar® to Gemzar® to keep his red cell count from dropping too low from radiation. That new chemo treatment only took about 60 minutes to drip in, and we were out of there! And the good news was that Larry had gained two pounds in the past week.

That Friday evening, we took off with my folks and niece to visit Dina in Madison. We had the best time.
One of our favorite summer activities in Madison was attending their famous Farmer's Market. It wraps around the entire block surrounding the State Capitol building in downtown Madison. We bought fresh flowers, herbs, plants, fresh spinach, strawberries, flatbreads, and our favorite cheese bread.

THE GIFT OF TODAY

That cheese bread was incredible! A warm loaf of round bread with red pepper flakes mixed into the batter, and wonderful melted, buttery cheese on the inside that drapes and strings everywhere as you pull the bread apart. The taste is indescribable, and just thinking about it makes my mouth water.

The next morning Larry and I were "greeters" for the 9:30 a.m. worship service at church—greeting and welcoming everyone as they arrived. Everyone made such a fuss over how good Larry looked. He was all dressed up and with that bald head, earring, suit and tie, he was just too handsome! He had an amusing comment for everyone he saw and had everyone smiling. He was an inspiration to those around him.

Later that day my dad and I planted 16 shrubs in the yard, eight Rose of Sharon and eight Forsythia bushes. They were pretty small, but would be great hedges some day. At least they were bigger than the trees we'd planted earlier in the month, which by the way, had already been run over by the lawn mower at least twice and didn't have a prayer of surviving.

We set up our firepot on the patio. (The only firepot we knew of with a personality. It's shaped like a person's head with the mouth as the opening for the firewood.) Dina came home for the day and asked if we could make s'mores, which we did. Then she and Larry took off for the golf course together. Dina didn't golf, she just liked driving the cart, and was a great cheerleader for her dad. While they were on the course together, apparently there was some discussion about her relationship with Matt, her boyfriend.

Larry told me much later that he informed Dina that Matt was not the right choice for a lifelong partner for her. I had practically beaten my head against the wall trying to make that point with her, and Larry finally pointed out to me one day that the more I pushed in that direction, the more she would defend him. And of course, he was right. He asked me not to say another word about it to her. *Not an easy task for me.* But I did as he asked. Discovering that he had this discussion with her, surprised me. But when her dad spoke, it was different. It was like the old investment commercials where a group of people are talking and when this one guy opens his mouth to speak, everyone stops to listen. Dina really took what he said to heart.

The next morning my parents returned home to Arkansas. It was difficult to say goodbye. It was so wonderful to have family there to help focus on something other than chemo, radiation and lab values. They were a tremendous help to Larry and me, and it was very emotional to watch them leave. The good news was that my sister and her family were arriving in a few days and would stay over the weekend. That gave us something to look forward to.

Larry had now completed eleven radiation treatments and still had a rasp in his voice. The radiation oncologist said he might have that for up to a year. Larry considered that bad news. I guess it was just a difference in the way we looked at things. When she said that, all I could think was, *Hallelujah! She's predicting he will still BE here in a year.*

In an attempt to ease the tension, I told him that with his bald head, earring and raspy voice, if we got him some funky clothes he could probably be a back-up singer for Rod Stewart. He just rolled his eyes.

The radiation treatments had given him a sore spot deep inside that had affected his swallowing, so we went shopping for "soft food." These were the kinds of things Larry loved (mashed potatoes, noodles, tapioca pudding, etc.) We were indulging very differently now.

The shoulder pain had subsided since he was golfing less. Some days he was just too tired to play, and our summer heat and rain made

THE GIFT OF TODAY

it almost impossible. Larry was sleeping better, which allowed me to sleep better.

His attitude about the cancer was good. He just didn't want to dwell on it.

"I just want to live each day as normally as I possibly can," he said. "And whatever happens, happens. There's nothing I can do to change any of this, so why think about it? It's out of my control." *What a smart man!*

As much as I enjoyed having my sister, brother-in-law and their three children stay with us, I realized afterward that adding five people to our household at that time was hard on Larry. I believe I was selfishly thinking about how nice it would be to have family members there to talk and visit with, and not about the rest and quiet that Larry needed. He wasn't used to the activity levels of three young children. They were very well-behaved, but wanted to play and have fun. Let's face it, children make noise. I knew he appreciated their visit and had always loved Bobbie. But, he was ready for some solitude. After their departure, I found him sound asleep in front of the fireplace—something he hadn't been able to do comfortably for a few days.

It was funny because I had a feeling that Bobbie tried to prepare her kids that Uncle Larry would look different than the last time they'd seen him. When they arrived, her four-year old son Nathan looked at my husband with the wide-eyed innocence of a child, and said shyly, "Hi Uncle Larry. You look the same." We all chuckled because he recognized that something was very different but didn't want to offend his Uncle Larry. Out of the mouths of babes.

"Dear Lord, I am thankful for the rain that waters my flowers and trees, makes the grass green and helps us to conserve water. I am grateful for people who care, dear friends, fulfilling work and the chance to make a difference in so many lives; thank you for the roof over my head, my wonderful husband and daughter, my parents

who drove so many long hours to be here and for their safe return home. Thank you for my sister and her family who realized how much we needed to be with them, for my health and for the blessings that have been granted to us. I thank You, God, for Larry's response to treatment, for his great attitude, and for giving us the ability to smile and laugh. It is rare to be granted so many gifts. It would be a pity not to recognize them. Rejoice! Again, I say rejoice. Amen."

CHAPTER TWELVE

A Roller Coaster of Events

I've heard it said that in order for life to be in balance, there has to be good and bad. I've read that in order for us to appreciate joy in our lives, we have to experience pain. So it was for the next couple of months.

For several years I had participated in the local Relay for Life event to raise money for cancer research and awareness. Relay for Life participants formed teams and canvassed for pledges and donations to the American Cancer Society. On the day of the event, at least one member of each team was represented on the walking track continuously, for 12 hours.

Larry never understood what that was all about. He couldn't understand why people walked around a track and thought it would make a difference in somebody else's life. In 2001, Larry walked for the first time in the Relay for Life as a cancer survivor, and let me tell you, it meant something to him. He walked alongside other men and women, many with bald heads and no eyebrows, who knew too well the war that cancer wages on the body and mind. He walked proudly, and I felt like he finally got it. And the best part was that he wasn't walking for himself, but to show others that he met his opponent with his head held high, and he was winning the battle. Dina and I were extremely proud of him.

The following morning I woke up to a horrible pain in my back that radiated up my neck. I didn't know if I had slept in an odd position or what had happened to me. I only knew that I could barely get out of bed.

This was one of my greatest fears—becoming sick or incapacitated during Larry's fight with cancer. Sometimes I felt guilty even thinking about my own health. But in order to take care of him, I had to be well. I couldn't afford to be laid up with everything that was going on.

I decided that working that neck and back would be the right thing to do. I took a warm shower and went outside to weed, spread ten bags of mulch and plant flowers. I took another warm shower and then did the grocery shopping. Finally, Larry and I attended our church's Saturday evening contemporary worship service. That night I took a couple anti-inflammatories. When I woke up Sunday morning, I was in the same pain.

I continued to believe I could not baby this thing. We played 18 holes of golf, with a cart (*thankfully*). After lunch we fished at the dam. The pain was tolerable so I just kept doing what I was doing—stubbornly refusing to take it easy.

By Monday morning, I could barely move. The pain had now radiated up the right side of my neck and into my right arm. I was in agony. I couldn't stand up straight and even the warm shower didn't help. I made it to work and noticed my supervisor standing in a similar position, only favoring the other side. When we stood next to each other, we looked like a pair of lopsided bookends. She had the same problem I did. She had an appointment with a chiropractor that morning, but I decided to tough it out, using ice and anti-inflammatories. A co-worker gave me an incredible backrub that helped, but only temporarily.

After four days, I gave in and saw a chiropractor. For several days I had ultrasound treatments to the area of the nerve root. I continued the

THE GIFT OF TODAY

heat, cold, painkillers, and stinky smelling lotions that are supposed to relieve muscle pain, all with little relief.

I finally decided to see a doctor, who gave me muscle relaxants, pain pills and steroids. I continued to have the same problem, but now I was so medicated, I didn't care! That continued for almost two weeks before the pain subsided. The doctor said I had contracted a virus that settled in my back. My supervisor's symptoms were the same and lasted as long as mine. When the day finally arrived that I could sit in a hard chair, raise my right arm without pain, and lift again, I was so grateful. Thank God that Larry's condition was stable while I was sick.

Following the most recent chest x-ray, Larry received a call from the hospital in late June saying that his tumor had "dramatically decreased in size." His last treatment was scheduled for June 28th and we couldn't imagine not having to drive to Rockford every day anymore. *What would we do with all that free time?*

Larry's voice seemed to last a little longer each day before it started getting raspy, and his throat was less irritated. His only problem was that he'd become very appealing to mosquitoes, flies, bees, ants and so on. He was constantly under attack it seemed, and because his immune system was so compromised, he got terrible welts from the least little bite or sting. He took Benadryl® nightly to keep the allergic reactions under control. It helped him sleep a little better, but not much. I couldn't believe how many nights he would waken during the wee hours of the morning. We also noticed a red streak up his arm where the chemo nurse had tried, three times, to start his IV line. So back he went on antibiotics. Just one more thing.

Being a one-car family, we talked about getting Larry some "wheels" so he could drive around town, and go to the golf course or out for coffee, while I had the car at work. We found a used, yellow moped that Larry loved. It was perfect for his needs, and gave us both a little more independence. The neighbors got such a charge out of watching him come barreling out the garage and down the driveway on that bike.

At Larry's last radiation treatment, they had a party for him. The staff wore masks and blew horns. There was a cake and they took a group picture. It was truly a celebration. He had to return in 30 days for a CT scan to get the exact dimensions of the tumor, and see the progress that had been made with the 30 radiation treatments. We were on pins and needles waiting for that day.

Dina had gotten a promotion at work, now had her own office, and told us that she was moving into her own apartment and splitting up with Matt. That was not just music, but rather a symphony to our ears. She had really started practicing her faith again and it made a difference in what she now saw in him.

The next weekend was July 4th, our 25th wedding anniversary. We celebrated by going to brunch with Dina in Madison. Later, we walked to a Mallards baseball game and enjoyed an incredibly elaborate fireworks display. The entire show was synchronized to music, from classical to rock. If a song came to the word "love" then heart-shaped fireworks burst in the sky. If it was about being "happy" or "smiling" then yellow smiley faces appeared. It was so awesome.

Saturday morning we enjoyed the wonderful Madison Farmer's Market. Then, we helped Dina choose a great little studio apartment in a nice area of town, less than a block from the beach. It was perfect for her.

Three weeks in a row, Larry's chemo appointment was postponed due to a low red blood count level. After the last chemo and all the radiation, his counts were not bouncing back. He started ProCrit® shots and IV iron to build up the red blood cells again. It took time

THE GIFT OF TODAY

for his body to react to the ProCrit®, but those shots prevented transfusions.

The second week in July, a neighbor who was recuperating from esophageal cancer treatments died suddenly at home. When his wife called 911, they managed to revive him, only to lose him again in the ambulance. Larry felt so bad that this man had gone through months of chemo, radiation and surgery, only to die suddenly. His doctor had told him that he was doing so well he didn't have to return for two months, and then this happened.

His wife thought he had beaten this disease. She now hoped that Larry would be the one to beat the cancer. We attended the funeral service but couldn't go to the widow's home afterward. It was just too hard. He died of a massive heart attack, which we learned is fairly common after extensive chemo and radiation treatments. *Could this happen to Larry?* It all hit so close to home.

Then, we were told that a friend's son who had been struggling with depression, committed suicide. He left behind a young wife and two small children. Larry and I were devastated. Here we were trying with every ounce of our being to keep Larry alive, and this young man who had so much to live for, took his own life. Isn't life ironic? That was also a very difficult funeral to attend. That poor young family felt abandoned by the person who was supposed to be their provider. My heart went out to them as I struggled to understand how someone could think that taking their life would not affect the other members of their family. I also wondered how people reached the point of feeling that desperate.

I began to think about what must go through a cancer patient's mind about living each day for that day only and not "planning" into the distant future. I decided that I didn't want these events to get Larry down and I wanted him to have something to look forward to. I prayed about it and then called Dina to ask her opinion about an idea. She was definitely in favor of proceeding, so I ran it past Larry.

My idea was for the three of us to go to Kauai, one of the Hawaiian islands, for the Christmas holiday. It would be our 25th anniversary and Christmas present to each other. I could see the excitement in his face, but he was also apprehensive.

"That's fine," he said. "We'll book this trip. But, if something goes wrong between now and then, promise me you'll find someone to take with you and Dina to Kauai. Don't let the trip go to waste."

I assured him that we would honor his wishes, but that HE would go with us. Nothing would happen.

Because we made the most of each day, never knowing if it was our last together, we looked at things differently than other people. We were living on the edge more, trying new things, venturing out of our comfort zone. It was exciting in a way. We had talked about going to Hawaii for a long time. *Why did we keep putting it off?* If we had a dream like that, it was our duty to pursue it. We continued to praise God for the beauty in each day, the opportunities before us, the rebirth of our faith and the serenity we had found—not in avoiding the storm, but in finding the peace within it.

On August 1, 2001, Larry went for his CT scan to determine the actual size of his tumor after all the treatments he'd received. Now remember, this tumor had been nine centimeters (about four inches), wrapped around his pulmonary artery and aorta, and inoperable. We knew his swallowing, voice quality, and comfort level had improved.

We expected a good report, but we never expected this.

When the radiation oncologist came in the room and began talking with us, we saw her lip quiver. She explained that under normal circumstances, after 30 treatments and then waiting 30 days, they expected the tumor to be approximately one-half the size.

Larry's tumor was GONE! YES, it was GONE! It had to be at

THE GIFT OF TODAY

least the size of a small pea to show up on the CT scan, and there was nothing there.

She told Larry he was the model patient. She was truly in awe of him because this was so rare! He never complained, he never balked at anything, he came in with a smile and left with one, and he was always kind to the staff. She was so happy for him.

I truly believe that prayer and a positive attitude have everything to do with recuperation. Larry and I never looked back or questioned why he developed cancer. We stared every day in the face and prayed. What power there is in prayer! Angels watched over us continuously and we felt their presence. Sometimes I felt God was squeezing us so tightly to make certain we knew He was there with us. *How do people manage illness without faith? I will never understand that.* Larry and I openly wept upon receiving the news. It was God's almighty hand.

This incredible news should be celebrated. We called our co-workers, neighbors, and friends. We asked everyone to spread the word and come to our house that evening for a party. Appetizers and champagne for everyone! People started arriving at 3:00 and never stopped until 8:00 p.m. There was a steady stream of people coming and going all evening. We were on cloud nine. There was laughter, tears, screams of joy and hugs to be shared. Dina sobbed with joy and relief when we told her. We felt so bad that she wasn't there to share in our celebration in person, but just knowing that things were improving that much gave her a sense of peace.

Two days later, Larry and I met with the oncologist to review his new treatment plan. The cancer cells were already in his pleural fluid so we knew he was not rid of the cancer, just the lung tumor. When the oncologist looked at his CT, she thought she had the wrong one. It was incredible to her too. She ordered two more cycles (two more months) of chemo to keep the pleural fluid levels down. We could live with that. Larry asked if this series of events would prolong his life. Her response was, "Maybe a month. None of us has a handle for sure on that."

At first he looked disappointed. But she went on to assure him that a timeline is not cast in concrete.

"Some people are given six months to live and go on for years. Others are told they have five or six years and are gone in months," she explained. "Much of it has to do with attitude and following the treatment plan. Don't dwell on that," she continued. "Just enjoy each day." (Which we were doing.)

Larry really surprised me then. He asked the doctor for Viagra. He explained that because of his low blood counts, we had not been able to make love since February. We were going away to celebrate our news and he thought...

She gave him some samples, but smiled and said he wouldn't need them.

On the way home, we shopped for new summer clothes for Larry. He would need them for a week in Door County (our favorite vacation spot) and for the Kauai trip in December. We really splurged. He got new shorts, shoes, shirts, and never balked once. He was having the time of his life. My husband, who believed that if you couldn't get what you needed at Farm & Fleet, Menards or the local hardware store, was picking out clothes. Unbelievable!

We drove through Madison on the way up to Door County so that we could see Dina. She was so thrilled to see her dad and vice versa. They hugged and laughed and cried together.

It was an incredible week in Door County. We saw some of the most beautiful sunsets we had ever seen. And, for the first time since February, my husband was able to make love to me. The doctor was right—he didn't need the pills!

The weather was unbearably hot during our stay. Larry laughed and shook his head in disbelief when I actually asked one day if we could leave one of the stores because I was too hot to shop. "I never thought I would live long enough to hear that!" he commented.

THE GIFT OF TODAY

We saw plays, took hikes, held hands, took a ferry boat to the island for a tour, played golf, ate at wonderful restaurants, toured the winery and made passionate love. It was fantastic!

We returned home to an enthusiastic reception from our precious little dog, Molly, and with happy memories that would stay with me, and bring comfort, for years to come.

With this new lease on life, even small things brought pleasure. After 23-plus years of service, our old Sears lawn mower died. Although Larry insisted that he could fix it, I insisted that it was time to give it a decent burial. After much discussion, we were on our way to Sears. We could have bought another brand, but when a mower lasts 23 years, why would we?

We came home with a 21 horsepower riding lawn mower with automatic transmission. Larry was excited about the deep deck and the CUPHOLDER! I was just glad to see him excited.

"Dear God, I come to You today with a heart that wants to explode from the joy within it. I know that Your hand has brought about the events we have experienced and I thank You for Your gracious mercy and love. I thank You for looking past the person I am sometimes, and guiding me to be better. I thank you for giving me this time with my husband that is so special, so wonderful, and so precious. I thank You for employers that have stood by us through all of this and never complained. They never made us feel that anything but Larry's health was important. I thank you for a daughter that loves us and has come to know You again. I thank you for taking away my pain and helping me to be physically strong again. I know we cannot change the past and we can make our present pretty miserable by worrying about the future, Lord, so we are giving it to You... After all, you'll be up all night anyway! To God be the Glory! Amen."

CHAPTER THIRTEEN

The Surprise Party

In August, I began plotting and planning. Larry's 75th birthday was in December. I knew that with the Kauai trip and the Christmas holiday, December would be too hectic for a birthday party. I wanted to surprise him with a bang-up birthday and the only way to do it was to have it early. I talked with friends and one of our neighbors, Karen, who offered to host the party on September 9th. I couldn't believe it. I explained that there might be 80 people, but she didn't care. I told her that I wanted to have a backyard party, and she said that was fine.

Karen worked at the same nursing home as Larry, and had admired his strength during the long months of treatment. They had enjoyed working together on the backstage crew for the local Performing Arts Guild. I knew she wanted to do something special for him, but her kindness was still overwhelming.

I had to keep things moving along on a daily basis so that Larry didn't become suspicious, but there was a lot of work to do. Dina helped, long distance, by making the invitations on the computer and mailing them all out, asking each guest to bring a lawn chair. I ordered tons of food from the local grocery store deli and enough cake for an army.

THE GIFT OF TODAY

As the time approached, I began telling Larry that I had heard our neighbors, Rob and Karen, were having a big backyard party on September 9th. I figured he wouldn't become suspicious when he saw so many people gathering in their backyard. Parking was going to be a problem, though. Our backyards were back to back so I knew that some of the cars would spill over onto our street.

We continued on with our daily routines. Larry had his first new chemo treatment and developed intense itching within an hour. Benadryl® took care of it, and thankfully, there were no severe reactions.

In the midst of my planning for Larry's birthday, we celebrated my birthday on August 15. Larry sent me flowers and took me to dinner at a lovely restaurant. We had a wonderful time together. It was so good to see him dressed up, looking healthier and smiling. His appetite was back and we were so grateful. We looked at each other like newlyweds. It was incredible how our relationship had changed. We had stopped taking each other for granted and fallen in love all over again.

We went to visit one of our former neighbors, an 89-year old woman who had once been Dina's babysitter. What a treasure! I had never met anyone so independent and so faithful to the Lord. She lived simply, but was the most gracious lady I had ever met, with a tremendous wit and spirit. She was living out her days at home after being diagnosed with pancreatic cancer. Her grandson lived with her but wasn't there all the time, so the neighbors checked on her daily. She was considered Dina's "great grandmother" because of their special relationship. Every year she remembered Dina's birthday with a cake and gift. We reciprocated on her birthday and I know she loved the attention, especially from a girl Dina's age. She felt it was so special that Dina made time for her. Dina went with us to visit her that day. They took pictures together and it was the last time they spoke. She passed away a month or so later. It was a very sad funeral for us and we miss her terribly, but we were thankful for the gift of that loving relationship.

Larry continued to play the best golf of his life. He was putting up scores like 44 for nine holes. That was quite admirable. And, he swore he wasn't cheating! He was swinging the clubs and driving like never before. He golfed with a buddy from work in the Good Samaritan Tournament to benefit the nursing home. They won a round of golf at the Mt. Carroll Country Club. That worked out perfectly for me. Each time he went golfing, I got a few more things done for his surprise party. It was coming along quite well.

Tuesday, September 4, Larry was scheduled for a "double whammy" chemo treatment, or so we thought. We arrived and sat in the waiting room for over an hour before realizing we were there on the wrong day. Unbelievable! We were a day early. There was no way to squeeze us in because it was a three-hour appointment, so we had no choice but to leave and return the next day. With the commute to Rockford, plus waiting, it was more than three hours wasted! My employer was very understanding, but I had to make up all the hours missed, so it was just harder on me.

During this time I investigated the possibility of giving Larry his ProCrit® shots at home (with the blessing of the Insurance Company). When they agreed to let me administer the ProCrit®, it saved us an 80-mile round trip to Rockford and it saved the insurance company money. The cost of the injection alone was $1,700.00. When I gave it, the insurance company no longer had to pay an administration fee to the clinic. *Thank God for insurance.*

We returned the next day for what turned out to be a rat race. Everyone was running behind, their stress levels were overwhelming, and the appointment took four-and-one-half hours instead of three. I think it was God's way of slowing us down. We had to take a deep

THE GIFT OF TODAY

breath, sit and relax. There was nothing else to do. It was a good time to practice the gift of patience that we had relearned over the months.

The weekend of the party finally arrived and I was so nervous. We had invited 82 people! My sister Cathy and her husband Michael came for the weekend to help distract Larry and attend the party. In their words, they needed to "get out of Dodge"…take a break from routine.

Saturday evening we went out for dinner to a lovely Italian restaurant and tried to look nonchalant about everything. Larry suspected nothing! Dina came home for the weekend and was a tremendous help with some of the preparations.

The morning of the party I woke up to overcast skies. By 9:00 a.m., it was pouring rain. I don't just mean a little rain shower; it was coming down in buckets. I had never seen it rain that hard. This was supposed to be a backyard party. Even if it stopped raining and the sun shone in all its glory, the ground would have been too soggy. There was no way we could have a party in the yard.

I ran upstairs and called Karen from inside the closet, so Larry wouldn't hear.

"What are we going to do!" I wailed in a stage whisper.

"We'll just move the party indoors," she replied practically.

"INDOORS? There are 82 people invited to this party! How can we have it indoors?"

Karen never got flustered. "We'll manage and everyone will have a great time. Don't worry." She only had two questions. How was *I* going to get over there, especially with company at my house, and how we were going to get Larry there?

I had to think fast. Cathy and I would say we were going shopping and that's when we'd pick up the food and take it to the party. In order to get Larry there, all she needed to do was call him at home at the appropriate moment, and say that she had a house full of people and her toilet was overflowing. I guaranteed that he would be there in a flash. After all, he was a maintenance man! She didn't think it would work. I knew it would.

As the time for our sneaky departure approached, Larry and my brother-in-law, Michael, became engrossed in a football game on TV. I announced that Dina, Cathy and I were going uptown to a little gift shop. They were so engrossed in the game, they barely noticed when we left. We drove to the grocery store and picked up all the cakes, food and drinks. We delivered all the food to Karen and Rob's house and guests soon began arriving. Some people stayed home as a result of the weather, but over 65 brave souls and loyal friends attended.

When the timing seemed perfect, Karen called our house. Larry answered the phone. In a panicky voice she asked if he would PLEASE help her out because she was having a party and her toilet began overflowing. Larry responded just as I knew he would. "Oh gosh, I'll be right there!"

We all watched from the windows as my husband sprinted out the back door, plunger in hand, with Michael in hot pursuit. He was running through our yards and splashing in water up to his ankles. We were hysterical. My neighbors caught the entire thing on video and later Larry laughed so hard while watching it that he cried.

Karen met him at the door and when she opened it, he pushed his way in and asked where the toilet was that needed plunging. We all darted out and yelled "SURPRISE!!! HAPPY BIRTHDAY!!!" The poor guy grabbed his chest and the color drained from his face. For a moment, he scared me. Then he looked around the room, saw me, Dina, his son, daughter-in-law, all our dear friends, and became very emotional. He was absolutely shocked.

It was the perfect surprise party. And, our neighbor's house was ideal. They had a beautiful three-season room in the back, their rooms were large, and the flow of the rooms never made anyone feel left out

THE GIFT OF TODAY

or crowded. It worked out flawlessly, and Larry was smiles from ear to ear.

In honor of his 75th birthday he received great gag gifts—a walking cane with a horn and rear view mirror, trick golf balls, a Hawaiian lei filled with miniature bottles of rum, and so on. Dina gave him a pair of tropical print swim trunks for Kauai. When he opened the box he held them up to himself and pretended to do the hula. I couldn't believe what a ham he was being.

Everyone was so supportive to come out in that horrible weather to give him such a special day. He was having the most incredible time and even though the weather kept us from being outdoors, the rain didn't dampen our spirits one bit! We had copious amounts of food, but the Italian in me always thought, b*etter too much than not enough.* We had broasted chicken, Italian beef sandwiches, pasta salads, baked beans, potato salad, relish trays, fruit salad, and cake.

Dina stayed until the following day so she could help clean up. We were all exhausted, but she was up before dawn on Monday and drove straight from our house to work in Madison. We sent her home with a cooler full of food that lasted at least a week. Every child appreciates that!

Thank God for neighbors like ours, for a daughter who says, "Mom, what can I do to help you?" and for friends and family who were there when we needed them. It was an awesome experience for Larry.

"Heavenly Father, I don't know how to thank you for allowing this to work out in the midst of pouring rain today. You have given us an incredible daughter and neighbors that are selfless. How many people would consider having a party for someone else and open their home to 65 people in the midst of a rainstorm? We are so blessed! You are the most awesome God and I am so lucky to know You personally. I'm glad I can talk to You about anything and that You are always there to listen. I can't express the love I have for You for giving my husband

new life. It was so good to have this time with friends and family, especially Cathy and Mike. Thank you for sending these wonderful angels to us. We are so appreciative. You are so great! I ask only that you continue to wrap Your arms around us, our family and dear friends, and keep us all safe. In Jesus' holy name I pray. Amen."

CHAPTER FOURTEEN

September 11, 2001

*W*hat can I say about that day that hasn't already been said? We were so busy getting ready for Larry's chemo appointment that morning that we didn't realize what was going on in the world. As Larry sat in the "chemo chair," we turned on the TV to catch up on news. To our shock and dismay, many Americans were losing their lives at the hands of terrorists. We could not believe the devastation in New York City and elsewhere as lives, buildings and aircraft were intentionally destroyed.

Witnessing the planes crash into the Twin Towers over and over again was a horrific emotional experience. I didn't want to believe that human beings were capable of this.

Again we thought about the irony of life. Here we were, sitting in a hospital, feeding poison into my husband's veins in an attempt to kill off this disease and keep him alive. Yet there were people who thought so little of life that they were willing to give up their own and take thousands of others with them.

I knew that God had a purpose for all of this, whether it was to unite this country or make us aware of what was REALLY important in our lives. I also knew we would emerge a stronger nation because of it.

It was the worst thing I had seen in my lifetime, and I prayed that we would join together behind our President and Congress to bring swift justice not only to those responsible, but to those who harbored the terrorists. We prayed for the families of those who were killed, for the injured, and for those brave enough to enter the buildings with the sole purpose of saving another life—even if it meant risking their own.

We prayed for our leaders to make the right decisions about how to deal with this kind of terrorist activity, and that all US citizens would realize that no American pilot could have possibly flown a plane full of people into the World Trade Center.

We prayed for the pilots who surely experienced their hell that day at the hands of terrorists. We prayed for the airlines that obviously had breeches in security. And, we prayed that this would awaken our nation to realize just how vulnerable we really were.

We prayed for the passengers onboard the planes, who were held captive by people with no regard for human life. We saw hero after hero—firemen, medical staff, policemen and every day citizens—come to the aid of their fellow man. It was something to see and take pride in.

We also witnessed the panic over reports that gasoline would rise in price, and watched people hoard gasoline in containers before local stations raised the price thirty cents per gallon. We prayed that greed would not play a role in this already tragic situation.

We gave thanks that all members of our families and close friends were accounted for and safe. We gave thanks that a nuclear plant ten miles away was not targeted. And we prayed that this type of activity would be extinguished quickly so everyone would soon know peace.

We sobbed along with the nurses and other patients in the chemo area that day because the despair and destruction was too much to bear. It was almost a relief when we had to leave the hospital and remove ourselves from the TV for a while. It was impossible not to watch when the television was right there.

THE GIFT OF TODAY

When Larry was diagnosed with cancer there was an incredible sense of loss that smothered us both. We were literally brought to our knees and didn't look at life the same way anymore. We made the most of each moment and decided not to postpone what we really wanted to do. We worried less about petty things and tried to focus on what was REALLY important. Surprisingly, those things were very basic and became so clear. They were not material things, but rather, the gifts of faith, hope and love.

I really felt with the World Trade Center crisis, that our country had been diagnosed with an autoimmune disorder. We had actually turned on ourselves and exposed our vulnerabilities. It left us with a very weakened immune system.

At that very moment, cancer struck—cancer in the form of terrorists. We lived as very self-centered individuals; not caring deeply about one another or this country and it was obvious to our enemies. We were a diseased nation, fighting amongst ourselves about political issues, values, or the lack of them, and morality had sunk to new lows. We had become an extremely materialistic nation. The terrorists saw our vulnerability and attacked. Fortunately, chemotherapy was administered in the form of Americans coming together in patriotism and love for one another to destroy the disease and go to war to fight the enemy and protect the body from further invasion.

The sad part about chemotherapy, is that "good cells" or "good people" lose their lives in the process. It was time to return to a different value system and put faith back into our God (the Great Oncologist) who would guide us to a new treatment plan and new life. It was our only hope.

That weekend, Larry and I drove to Madison to visit Dina and were so impressed with the spirit that had come alive in the nation. As we approached a major stoplight, two young men waved an American flag and a huge sign that read, *"Honk if you love America!"* The noise level of car horns at that intersection was almost deafening. We passed a lemonade stand operated by a family in front of their home. The children were waving flags and the parents were draped in red, white and blue. They were raising money to send to World Trade Center survivors. This was the kind of patriotism we needed in our country again.

That evening, we attended a church service in honor of the World Trade Center survivors and those who lost their lives. There were over 600 people at that church, whose usual attendance was about 200. The songs were spiritual and patriotic, and the walls were ringing with enthusiasm for the music and for the American people. What a shame that it took a tragedy of this magnitude for us, as a people, to act accordingly.

We continued our weekend in Madison, mainly just enjoying quality time together and beautiful fall weather.

"Lord, thank You for the opportunity to be together today and for the beautiful weather. Thank you for keeping us safe. I don't understand the series of events that unfolded this week, but I know that You do. My prayer is that the world will soon know peace and that we will come together as a nation with new priorities and new values. I pray that we will open our hearts to You and that we will be refreshed with a new Spirit.

Lord, I ask You to forgive me for not always putting You first in my life and for making everything else more important. May I realize the depth of your love and the gift of salvation that is mine simply for putting my faith in You. I am so blessed! Grant us a peaceful week with time for reflection and thanksgiving. Give me the gift of compassion to help in whatever way I am able with this tragedy our country has experienced. Help us to heal and bring us the peace that only You can give. These things I pray in Jesus' name. Amen."

CHAPTER FIFTEEN

A New Wrinkle

As September and October rolled by, we were pleasantly surprised that Larry's blood levels stabilized and his appetite increased. He was receiving IV iron and it tremendously improved his energy level.

He was doing so well that I agreed to help with a slumber party at work for our female consumers, (women with developmental disabilities). A co-worker and I had the idea of having a slumber party at work—doing make-overs on each other and all the girly things that teenagers do at slumber parties, even though our party-goers would be in their 30's, 40's and 50's. Everything was going along well enough at home that I could stay away overnight and know that Larry was fine. He thought it was a great idea and would give me a chance to have a little fun "with the girls."

The consumers had a great time applying make-up to the staff and each other. We looked like something straight out of the 70's with our teased hair, pale pink lipstick and white eye shadow. We polished each other's fingernails and acted just plain silly. We ordered pizza and then stuffed ourselves with homemade cheesecake. We danced, watched a movie, laughed, told jokes, laughed, sang and laughed some more. Everyone settled down around 11 p.m. (early for a girls' slumber party). The next morning after an equally unhealthy breakfast, we headed home. It was a good break for me. And I really think Larry enjoyed an evening alone without me doing my "caregiver thing."

We continued to plan our Christmas trip to the Island of Kauai and it was getting very exciting. By Thanksgiving we had purchased all of the little travel size necessities like toothpaste, shaving gel and mouthwash, as well as disposable razors, disposable cameras, pill organizers and acetaminophen. We were warned not to wait to purchase items like those on the island, because the cost was so outrageous. All the arrangements were made for airfare, hotel and rental car. It would be our first trip flying over the ocean, and because of my fear of water, I needed something from the doctor to calm my nerves on the plane. That phone call was added to the "must do" list as the time drew nearer.

Besides returning to work, Larry had been golfing and bowling and really enjoying himself the last several months. During the first week of December, however, he began complaining of lower back pain and immediately panicked.

"The cancer has moved to my bones. I just know it," he told me one morning with a horrified look on his face.

"Larry, there are lots of reasons that you might have back pain. Let's not panic and think 'cancer' right away. Maybe you just moved the wrong way and twisted something. Or maybe it's a little arthritis."

"I can't sleep well all of a sudden and a little arthritis shouldn't keep me awake at night," he answered.

I could certainly see that he was concerned. Of course, when you're battling cancer every pain and ache makes you fearful. I wondered, though, if it was just a bad case of nerves thinking about being so far away from home in case something happened.

We tried various over the counter medications for pain, sleep, and even prescription pain pills, but nothing helped. I wanted to put his fears to rest so I called the oncologist and explained what was

THE GIFT OF TODAY

happening. She immediately ordered a bone scan since we were leaving on our trip in less than three weeks. I wanted him to be comfortable and at peace for this trip. We put out a plea to all our friends and family via e-mail to pray that no cancer would be found on Larry's scan.

"*Ask and it will be given to you; seek and you will find; knock and the door will be opened to you.*" *(Matthew 7:7)*

We were definitely knocking. I knew it would be the trip of a lifetime if Larry could relax and enjoy it.

Two days later, we were at the hospital for his early morning bone scan. First, he was injected with dye. Then there was a two-hour wait during which time he had to drink six large glasses of water. He also had extensive blood work drawn and full back x-rays. It was a very long morning and we walked back and forth from the clinic to the hospital so much that we logged 1.8 miles, according to the marked walking path. But that sure beat sitting around all morning.

Two long days passed with no news about the scan, blood work or x-rays. I was starting to get a little impatient. Over the counter anti-inflammatories were getting him through the nights but I wanted to find out what was going on so that we could relieve his pain and anxiety.

Finally a nurse called with results. X-rays showed slight bulging of the discs, slight curvature of the spine and degenerative disc disease. All the things that go with old age! Wow, did I give him a hard time about that! I told him the good news was that there was no cancer in the bone. The bad news was…. He was OLD! I won't repeat his response. Actually, he had what was known as "golfers back." *Hmmmm, imagine that!* The oncologist ordered a strong anti-inflammatory prescription that he started the very next day.

In the midst of all this I received an hysterical telephone call from Larry's daughter-in-law. Larry's oldest son, Les, (52 years old) had been diagnosed with prostate cancer. Biopsies revealed that it was malignant, Stages III and IV. During the biopsies they removed several bleeding polyps from his colon. He chose to treat it aggressively but decided to undergo surgery after Christmas so that he could enjoy the holidays with his wife and 14-year old daughter.

When Larry came home from doing maintenance checks at the nursing home that morning, I told him about the phone call. He was devastated. I hated to tell him and I hated that there was more cancer so close to him. He couldn't believe what a pattern cancer had become in his family. Larry's parents both died of cancer, his mother passing away when he was only eleven years old. He was unsure of her exact diagnosis, only remembering that it was something "below her waist." When Larry was 33 his dad died of cancer—possibly cancer of the stomach. He had been a heavy smoker and Larry remembered him asking for a cigarette as he lay in pain in the hospital. Larry would light it for him and hold it to his mouth so that he could smoke. He just couldn't refuse a dying man what he wanted most.

Larry needed to talk to his son. He called and asked if we could drive into their Chicago suburb to see them the next day. Les was so happy to hear his dad's voice. I know he was touched that we wanted to be there to comfort him. They lived about 75 miles away and we just hoped that the Midwest winter would not rear its ugly head while we traveled there and back.

When we arrived at Les' home, the house was closed up, blinds were drawn, and the family was walking around with that look of total shock that comes with an unexpected cancer diagnosis. Larry's daughter-in-law, Judy, had obviously been crying and it was very depressing. We gave everyone a hug, then sat down and began talking about what was happening. Eventually, we started showing them pictures of Larry's surprise 75th birthday party, some pictures from a recent wedding and before we knew it, everyone was laughing. They

THE GIFT OF TODAY

started opening blinds and letting a little light into that gloomy house. They even agreed to join us for a relaxing dinner out. For one day at least, they stopped worrying about their troubles. We reassured them both that we had some great connections for prayer and had put them on our prayer chain at church. I'm not sure if they believed in the power of prayer, but we knew it had seen us through many experiences in our lives that we would have never survived on our own. God had been there for us at every turn.

We were now seven days away from our trip to Kauai. It had been a very eventful December with Les' cancer, Larry's back pain and preparing for vacation. Dina's new boyfriend of the past couple months, Adam, had agreed to house sit for us and take care of our beloved dog, Molly. Adam had also agreed to drive us to O'Hare Airport in our car and pick us up in a week. He was thrilled to drive our black Lincoln Continental with leather seats, a 6-CD changer and power moon roof. It didn't take much arm twisting! We were delighted not to board Molly in a kennel and to have someone look after our home. We paid him for his efforts so it was a win-win situation for everyone.

My prayer that day was this,
"Lord, I thank you for the incredibly unseasonable weather You have blessed us with this week and I thank you that we are safe and have food, shelter and clothing. We take so many things for granted in our daily lives. These are all gifts from You that we are so grateful for. I thank you for Larry's test results that showed no cancer in his bones, and for blood values that remain stable as we prepare to leave for our vacation. I thank you for a daughter that You have entrusted us with, that becomes more beautiful with each passing day. I thank you for friends and family who believe in the power of prayer and have prayed endlessly for Larry's health and for our wellbeing. I ask at this time that You wrap your arms around Larry's son who has been diagnosed with advanced stage cancer. I ask that You keep

Dianne Klancir

his condition from progressing any further until he can be operated on and that you guide his surgeon's hands to perform the operation successfully and rid his body of this ugly disease. I ask that You give strength to his wife and daughter as they try to accept this news. I ask for strength for Larry as I believe this is harder on him than facing his own cancer. Please Lord, give Larry some peace with the news that his cancer has not advanced to his bones and help him to relax and enjoy this family vacation we are about to embark upon. I ask for safe travel for our family, and I thank You for the gift of Adam who willingly has agreed to transport us to and from the airport. Please guide his travel and keep him safe. I ask these things in your Son Jesus' precious and holy name. Amen."

CHAPTER SIXTEEN

Mele Kalikimaka
(Merry Christmas in Hawaiian)

The time had finally arrived for our departure to Kauai. It was 6:00 a.m. on December 23, 2001. I could hardly believe we were going. I yearned to see more excitement on Larry's face so that I knew he was really up for this, but he was rarely the type to openly express his emotions. He always felt I got excited enough for both of us. I guess I had a passion for certain things and had trouble hiding my feelings.

Between the discomfort he had been experiencing and the news he received about his son, he had mixed emotions about leaving for this trip, but knew there was no backing out now. My head was spinning a mile a minute wondering if I was forgetting anything vital. I must have checked the suitcases at least three times to make sure I had all Larry's medications, the reservation papers, and the e-tickets we needed to pick up our boarding passes at the airport.

Dina and her boyfriend were busy making eyes at each other, and while I knew she was excited about being with us in Kauai for Christmas, it was equally hard on her not to be with him for the holiday.

Dianne Klancir

Although Adam and Dina had only dated for a few months, they'd known each other since junior high. Adam was considerate, nice looking and genuinely enjoyed spending time with our family. He lived about an hour away from Dina and drove to Madison at least twice a week to see her. Adam had served in the Army for four years and was now in the Reserves, with about four years under his belt. We were always concerned that if our country went to war because of the terrorist issues, he could be deployed. We tried not to think about that any more than necessary. Although we didn't think of this as a serious relationship yet, we did care about Adam, and always made him feel welcome. We truly appreciated that he was driving us, and would watch our home and Molly while we were gone. I imagine that it also made him feel closer to Dina, whom he was going to miss terribly. But, there would be other holidays they could spend together. This one was for the three of us—it was time we needed together.

It was still dark as we left the house. The usual blanket of snow that covers the Midwest in December was absent, and at 6:00 a.m. traffic toward the airport was moving along well. It was almost a two-hour drive to O'Hare Airport in Chicago. Larry allowed Adam to drive so he could just rest comfortably in the back seat. *Yeah, right.* I saw him watching Adam like a hawk. The Lincoln was Larry's baby and he didn't want any mishandling of that vehicle. I kept wishing there was something else I could have done to make Larry more comfortable, and I prayed that his pain would subside with the warm temperatures and new medication.

As we arrived at the airport, we left Adam behind. There was no point in parking the car and walking a few feet with us before we had to separate. It was a difficult goodbye for Dina, but I knew they would probably talk to each other on cell phones at least fifty times that week. Thank God for cell phones and free minutes!

We headed for the United terminal check-in area. The lines had already begun forming at the security gates and it was a rather lengthy

THE GIFT OF TODAY

process to get bags checked. Because it was a holiday and passengers were bringing wrapped packages and extra luggage, the process seemed rather tedious, but everyone was in good spirits and that helped. Even the airport personnel were smiling until Dina and I placed our things on the conveyor belt and they passed through the x-ray camera. The buzzers sent off a deafening sound all around us. Their expressions changed and it seemed that we were no longer looked at as holiday travelers, but rather as potential terrorists. My purse was thoroughly checked and I had forgotten to remove my nursing scissors (not exactly a deadly weapon), which I had carried since I was in nurse's training eleven years earlier. I convinced them that there wasn't one harmful thing I could do with those and they agreed to let me keep them. Then, they searched our carry-on bag and confiscated Larry's heavy-duty nail clippers and nail file. The National Guard soldier was not smiling at us as those were removed. Dina's backpack took forever because it had about twenty pockets, but nothing was removed. They finally decided that her batteries were what set off the alarms, and our belongings were allowed to pass. However, I was given a thorough body search by a female guard including the use of a wand, a search of my shoes and the underside of the waistband of my slacks. I guess I must have looked like a hijacker, but I didn't take it personally. We thanked them for being so thorough as we left for our gate. The people behind us in line were now less than enthused.

As we boarded the plane, a United 777, I marveled at the size. I had never seen a plane so huge. It's amazing to me that something that massive, filled with all those people, luggage, engines and fuel could not only leave the ground, but fly across the country. To me, the myriad of music channels available on my headphones and the personal TV on the back of the seat in front of me, seemed luxurious. We felt like royalty in economy class, but soon returned to reality when they served a box lunch of typical plane food. It was a smooth, uneventful flight for which we were grateful.

Dianne Klancir

We arrived in Los Angeles ten minutes earlier than expected. Larry seemed comfortable and actually began smiling and looking more relaxed. We stretched our legs for a while and before we knew it, we were boarding our flight to Kauai. This flight was a 757 plane and the seats were narrower, the TV screens were down the aisles, and if you were interested in the movie, everyone watched the same one. Dina sat two rows in front of us, as we were unable to get three seats together. It was a very turbulent flight and we were confined to our seats for the better part of the journey.

I was surprised that it took longer to fly from L.A. to Kauai, than it did to fly from Chicago to L.A. Kauai is the farthest island away from the mainland. I had taken my "relaxer" about one-half hour before we left the L.A. airport so that I would be almost sedated flying over the ocean. It helped a little, but the turbulence of that flight kept me somewhat alert. I was also concerned about Larry because the turbulence seemed to bother his back. He was nowhere near comfortable. We were actually served a meal on this flight with a choice of tantalizing chicken or luscious meat loaf. Between the bouncing of the plane and the narrow seats, it was difficult to eat a meal. Larry and I barely touched our food, not that I think we missed out on anything.

It was a relief when the plane landed at the Lihue airport in Kauai and we were able to stretch our legs. We had flown eleven hours that day. I was grateful we had taken a layover in L.A. and not flown straight through.

The Lihue airport is very small and it was almost dusk when we arrived. It was very overcast and humid, nothing like what I expected. I had always heard that the humidity was low in Hawaii and the climate was in the 60's in December. But, the beautiful flowers, palm trees and lush foliage were so shockingly different from the stark Midwestern landscape we'd left that morning, that we didn't even think about it. It was truly a paradise... and we hadn't even left the airport yet!

We picked up our rent-a-car and proceeded to navigate our way to our hotel, the Kauai Coconut Beach Resort in Kapaa.

THE GIFT OF TODAY

I was the designated driver on this trip and known far and wide for my gift of being "directionally-challenged." So it was interesting trying to navigate my way to the hotel in a strange place where darkness was setting in, but we made it—awed by the breathtaking scenery along the way, visible even at dusk.

Our resort was incredible. As we opened the car doors, we could hear the waves of the Pacific Ocean lapping up on shore just behind the hotel. The foliage was beautiful—palms swaying, gorgeous blooming tropical flowers, and the healthiest greenery I had ever seen! The next thing we noticed was that there were no doors at the entrance to our hotel. It was open to air. There were birds flying through the lobby and a huge, circular stained glass window with a wall of water in front of it that was so restful and divine. As we looked up, there were three levels to the hotel, and each one had wrought iron railings that overlooked the lobby. Beautiful vines were growing over each railing and everything looked so lavish. It literally took my breath away. Larry just stood with his mouth opened in amazement.

"Are you sure we can afford all this?" he asked. Dina had checked out everything on the lower level and returned with a commentary of "cool!!" There were two Christmas trees in the front lobby sporting hula dancers at the top where one would normally find angels or stars.

When we opened the door to our room we found two double beds, a huge entertainment center, a dorm-sized refrigerator, and beautiful wooden doors that slid open to reveal a balcony that overlooked the pool, entertainment bar and Pacific Ocean. It was unbelievable! We got our belongings settled and decided to take a look around. Dina, who had already surveyed the property, gave us a tour.

We went to the open air bar and each ordered a Hawaiian specialty drink and Coconut Shrimp. The service, drinks and food were wonderful. We enjoyed some Hawaiian music and dancers and then took a walk along the beach. The sand became difficult for Larry to walk on so he and I sat on a bench and Dina explored the beach independently. It was about 10:00 p.m. (now 2:00 a.m. Chicago time), 72 degrees, and the ocean waves looked almost luminous as they rolled in with the moon shining above. It was the most incredible thing to see! Dina called Adam to let him know we had arrived at the hotel safely, and those two missed each other already.

We returned to our hotel room to find a bottle of champagne, a gift from the hotel. Dina put it in the refrigerator and we decided to use it for a Christmas Eve toast the following evening. We were all looking forward to a good nights sleep as we had now been awake for almost 24 hours. As tired as we were, we were also excited to be here. We thanked God for safe travel, for medication that brought Larry relief from discomfort, and for the beautiful place we were given to celebrate Christ's birth. Here we were, in paradise, for Christmas. It was almost surreal.

I have never been one to sleep in or sleep long hours on my vacation. I could remember times in my youth when Saturday meant sleeping until 10:00 a.m. and then wasting away the day. That was ages ago. Occasionally, I slept until 7:30 a.m. on a weekend. It used to frustrate my husband, who believed that if you didn't get up at 5:30 a.m., you were missing out on half the day. That morning, Christmas Eve, I was the first one awake and it was still dark. The excitement of having a hotel room that faced east and the opportunity to see the sun rise over the Pacific Ocean from my balcony, with the gentle breeze rustling my hair, was something I did not want to miss. I wasn't disappointed. I had never seen anything so magnificent.

I was enchanted by the hustle and bustle around the hotel as the staff quietly groomed the grounds and cleaned the pool. The birds were singing and it was so peaceful and calm. It was just the way I had envisioned our vacation should be. We chose the Island of Kauai because of its reputation for quiet beauty and lack of commercialism. We needed to focus on the true meaning of the upcoming days in a

THE GIFT OF TODAY

quiet, spiritual place where Larry would find comfort from the cold temperatures. This was the perfect choice.

Dina slept in that morning so Larry and I went downstairs for our first Polynesian meal. We quickly developed a great relationship with papaya, guava and mango. There was so much fresh fruit available and it all tasted so good! The open-air restaurant allowed the birds to come right up to the tables. They were so used to tourists that people didn't even affect them.

When we returned to the room, Dina was sitting on the balcony writing postcards and told us that she had talked to Adam. Two inches of snow fell at our house and four inches fell in Madison, where Dina lived. We shivered from head to toe just to think about it, and then quickly dismissed it from our minds. It was 81 degrees in Kauai with 70 percent humidity. *Perfect!* Larry's back was uncomfortable that morning and he'd almost convinced himself to stay in the room and relax that day. But, Dina and I were not going to let him sit in front of a TV on a once-in-a-lifetime vacation.

We took a scenic drive up Highway 51 to 580 and saw the Opaeka Falls. We were able to pull off the road at one point and take pictures. Larry was in awe. Then we went to Smith Boat Tours down the road and booked a tour of the Fern Grotto. We were fortunate that there were others interested in going at the same time or they would have cancelled the tour. Hawaii's tourism had suffered since September 11th, and most days the boat tours would leave only a few times per day, rather than every half hour as before the terrorist attack.

The relaxing boat ride traveled down the Wailua River to the Fern Grotto. The tour was one-and-one-half hours long and very enjoyable. We were entertained with music and dancing by native men and women. At one point we all had to stand and attempt to learn the hula. What a riot! Even Larry with his sore back tried doing the hula.

At a certain point on the river, everyone disembarked. We walked to the grotto and admired the fern growth, were told about the varieties of ferns that thrive so beautifully there, and then walked inside and listened to our boat crew play "The Hawaiian Wedding Song." Many people are married at the Fern Grotto, and the acoustics are incredible. On the return boat ride, we were given the history of the area and the island in general. It was a very pleasant way to spend the morning.

Afterwards, we made reservations to take a 60-foot catamaran boat ride on Wednesday. It included breakfast and lunch, whale watching, snorkeling for treasures and diving. I had mixed emotions about that adventure, as I have never been a "water person." Larry and Dina adored the water, so I knew that even though Larry's back might not allow him to participate in some of the activities in the water, he would enjoy the ride as I would.

As we drove back to the hotel we discovered the Coconut Marketplace, with over 200 shops. I never thought I would find myself shopping, in my shorts no less, on Christmas Eve! Larry wanted to get me a silver chain with a single black pearl for Christmas and thought we would find a bargain on Kauai, but we were wrong. Instead, I got a crystal piece to add to my collection. It had a palm tree and an oyster opened to expose a beautiful white pearl. Into the base, which is a mirror, was etched "Kauai." Larry picked out a cap with the name of the island on it and a beautiful red Hawaiian print shirt. Dina chose a designer swimsuit. (And I have to admit there wasn't much to it, except for the price, but it was 50 percent off). That was her Christmas gift from the Island of Kauai.

For Christmas Eve dinner, we decided to attend our first luau. Our hotel advertised they had the "best luau on the island," so we took the bait. I had bought a flowered pink dress at the Marketplace and had matching pink sandals. Dina wore a beautiful, long, silk, flowered sundress, and Larry wore his new red floral shirt. Larry bought us each a fresh floral lei to go with our outfits as a special Christmas Eve treat. The fragrance was awesome and the flowers were indescribable.

THE GIFT OF TODAY

It's amazing the clothes a person will wear on vacation that they will not wear anywhere else, or the things they will do that they wouldn't be caught dead doing back home in front of friends, isn't it? Think of how much happier we would be if we acted like we were on vacation every day. I'll never understand why we don't enjoy this journey we call life more. Instead we treat ourselves to one or two weeks a year when we really let our hair down, try to cram it all in, and come back home exhausted, only to return to the drudgery of our everyday lives. Maybe we would be too worn out to function on a daily basis. But it sure sounds good to me.

As we entered the covered pavilion where the luau was being held, we were greeted by natives who placed shell necklaces around our necks. They handed us tropical drinks and seated us at tables. We were at a table very near the stage and the food. At first that made me a little nervous because I thought we would get picked to hula on stage or something equally embarrassing. Then I thought, *Oh what the heck. These people will never see me again. (See what I mean?!)* As it turned out, we didn't have to go on stage, but we were among the first to go through the buffet line. As we waited for the main entrée (the pig) we were entertained by two native Hawaiians playing guitars and singing, and scantily dressed Hawaiian girls dancing and making beautiful hand gestures. It was almost hypnotic. I glanced at Larry who had been very quiet, and he had a smile on his face that no one could have removed. It almost moved me to tears to see him so happy. My wish for this vacation was just for him to be able to forget about his pain and enjoy this beautiful place. Dina was even getting into the music and there were a couple of native young men who couldn't take their eyes off her.

Soon, the dinner was ready and the pig, which had been cooked in an Imu (in-ground oven), was uncovered. It had been covered in Ti and banana leaves to cook. It's a ritual that has to be experienced. There were lovely salads of all kinds, fried rice, beef and chicken teriyaki, mahi mahi, kahlua pig and turkey, baked sweet potatoes, poi, and various desserts. We enjoyed every morsel! Each table had pineapple boats filled with scrumptious fresh fruit, which just tasted better there. Following dinner there was more native dancing and entertainment. It was a hoot!

We returned to the room about 8:00 p.m. and exchanged a couple small Christmas gifts we had brought for each other. Larry gave Dina the book "Butterfly Kisses" which she has treasured. Dina called Adam that night to wish him a Merry Christmas and he was in tears, he missed her so much. Larry was ready for bed by 9:00 and I could see the look of exhaustion in his eyes.

He said wearily, "I'm so glad I didn't stay back here and we got to spend a great day together. I wouldn't have missed this for the world." Then he gave me a gentle kiss and hug and curled into bed. I gave him his medication and a backrub until he was asleep. I was so happy he was able to tolerate such a long day.

"Thank you God, for giving our family the opportunity to spend this day in such a glorious paradise. We thank You for the enormous blooming hibiscus and ginger plants that we had never seen before, for the magnificent sunrises and sunsets, for the perfect weather, for laughter and relief from pain. Thank you for helping us to realize that the birth of Jesus is just as special in the warmth and beauty of Kauai as it is in the cold Midwest with snow-covered pine trees and star-studded skies. Thank you for the angels You sent our way today that looked after Larry and helped him forget about cancer for a while. I ask only that my family continues to be protected and that Your angels continue their watch as we look to tomorrow, the birthday of your Son. In Jesus' name. Amen."

Sunrise Christmas morning was at 7:15 a.m. and I was on the balcony with my camera again. Larry and I had traveled many places to witness sunsets, but this was the first time we had photographed sunrises. It was spectacular as it rose over the ocean. I felt like we

THE GIFT OF TODAY

were the luckiest people on earth. Larry was in awe of the view from our balcony. He was up and in a great mood that morning. After we watched a fantastic Christmas choral concert on TV, we were off to another lavish breakfast buffet. We had discovered a new fruit juice— POG (papaya, orange and guava). We had fallen in love with POG. We discovered that POG is a great laxative, so we teased each other that there was a good reason the Hawaiians were always smiling.

Our waiter at breakfast had served us two days in a row, and would carry on long conversations with us about the island and the weather. (The expected high was 79 degrees that day!) He explained that the chickens and roosters that run loose all over the island are considered sacred and there was a fine if we hit one with our vehicle. He told us where to see beautiful peacocks and where the peacock crossings were located. He taught us about the beautiful white birds we had never seen before called Canyonbirds along the roadsides. He also told us that this was the first time in five years it had not rained in Kauai on Christmas Day and insisted that we brought the sunshine with us.

After breakfast we jumped into our rental car and drove to Waimea Canyon, better known as the Grand Canyon of the Pacific. The roads on the island were nicely paved as long as it was a main road. But some of the side roads were not as well maintained and had hairpin curves that were difficult to navigate. It took us an hour-and a-half to reach the lookout point, elevation 3,500 feet. It was breathtakingly beautiful and worth the drive. Returning, we detoured past Poi Pu Beach, which actually has very little beach, but vast amounts of black lava rock. The beach outside our hotel was much nicer.

We continued along the south shore to Spouting Horn, a beautiful geyser that shoots water up from the ground accompanied by a loud noise that sounds like an animal in the wild. It was so awesome! We had been warned that this time of year it didn't spout often. During our 45 minute visit there, it occurred three times. Unreal.

After a light lunch in Poi Pu that included fantastic mango smoothies, we returned to the hotel. Larry and Dina headed down to the ocean and hot tub. I went with them but brought a book and post cards. Larry said the hot tub felt great on his back but there were warnings not to stay in there too long because of the heat of the water. So, he went in and out, visiting with me or with other guests in the hot tub.

I was pleased to see him laughing out loud and having a great time. By the time we got back to the hotel room, he was complaining of back pain and said the medication he had taken that morning had worn off. I wanted him to take his medication at regular intervals to stay ahead of the pain, but he insisted he didn't want it if he didn't need it. He decided to delay taking the next dose so he could enjoy the champagne toast.

We put on our floral leis from the previous day and poured the champagne. He walked to the balcony and looked out at the ocean.

"Gosh, this is an unbelievable place, isn't it?" he asked. I came up behind him and gave him a hug.

"It certainly is. It's hard to believe we're really here. Isn't it incredible how you can get in a plane some place where it's freezing cold, travel a few hours and step out into 70-degree weather, palm trees, and the ocean? It still amazes me."

The three of us sat and talked about the joy of the day and what we wanted to do the rest of our stay in Kauai. Naturally, with a three-generation family we didn't always agree, and there were times when Dina got a little testy about the plans. I felt really torn at times. I knew that this was the trip of a lifetime for us as a family, and I wanted us to experience as much as we could on the island, just as Dina did, but I also had to consider that my husband was uncomfortable and try to figure out how to help him. I felt so helpless. I gave him the next dose of meds and hoped it would get him through until bedtime. It was a shame to be uncomfortable on Christmas and not be able to enjoy the events of the day.

THE GIFT OF TODAY

We readied ourselves for a 7:00 dinner at the elegant restaurant in our hotel, The Flying Lobster. They kept us waiting 15 minutes before they seated us, and Larry did not like waiting when he had a reservation anywhere. As soon as we were seated, he began fidgeting and saying he was uncomfortable in the chairs. I told him to give the medicine some time to work and thought he would feel better. The waiter, whose name was Moses, didn't appear for 20 minutes, then only brought our water and ordered our drinks. It was another 15 minutes before we received those and by the time he took our dinner order, they were out of what Larry wanted, which was turkey and stuffing. He complained and moaned to the waiter and really made quite a stink about it. He finally settled for ham, Dina had sautéed chicken with artichokes and I had the shrimp feast. We had to remind the waiter after quite a long while to bring our salads and soup, and when the food was finally delivered by another waiter, it was barely warm. It was not exactly the Christmas dinner we had hoped for.

Now, instead of the pain medicine working, Larry said he was more uncomfortable than ever and refused to eat his dinner. He didn't like the vegetables, he didn't like the ham, and he was just plain miserable. The evening went downhill very quickly. Dina and I had wonderful meals, albeit not as hot as we would have liked, but when Larry chose to leave, we said we'd meet him in the room when we were finished eating. I knew that sounded very cold, but we felt like he wasn't even willing to try. We wondered if some of these complaints of pain were more related to the fact that he was kept waiting and then didn't get what he wanted for dinner. And I was not going to let that ruin our Christmas.

Dina and I decided to postpone the catamaran trip until Friday in order to give Larry two days to rest. Maybe we had pushed him too hard the first couple days and he needed to recuperate. I gave Larry his bedtime medication, and both he and Dina were sound asleep by 10:00 p.m. I sat on the balcony and enjoyed the music from the open air bar.

Dianne Klancir

People were singing Christmas carols and having a wonderful time. For various reasons, it was a Christmas I would not soon forget.

"Heavenly Father, I thank You for the precious gift of your Son, Jesus, and for the beauty of this day. I ask that You forgive my impatience with my husband today, and that You give me the strength to take care of Larry and provide the love and compassion that a good wife should possess. I ask You for the wisdom and the right words to say in order to keep peace in my family. I'm sure Larry and Dina get frustrated with me at times as I can be very stubborn and strong-willed. Lord, please soften my heart and help me to know the right things to do. I ask for Your angels to continue to be with us and that You fill us with the Spirit that is Christmas. Please Lord, keep us from saying harsh things to each other and help us to love each other as You love us. I pray these things in your Son's name. Amen."

The next day was Wednesday. I awoke before 6:00 a.m. knowing that we had to change the reservation for the catamaran trip. Larry said he had a very restless night. I must have slept soundly not to have heard or felt him moving around. I finally reached the tour company and asked if we could reschedule to Friday or if we would lose our money. Those tours were not cheap. They were willing to let us reschedule, but warned that the weather and wave report for Thursday and Friday was much worse than Wednesday, and encouraged us to go that day. Larry looked outside at the ocean and decided that the water looked too rough for him to make the trip. He was concerned he might become nauseated and vomit, which in turn would worsen the pain in his back. I could understand that thinking, but there I was again, left in the middle as to what to do. And I was not the person who liked the water. Larry and Dina were the water lovers. *If he felt the water was too rough for him, should I be going?* I was torn. Dina was determined she didn't want to leave Kauai without taking this trip and seeing whale, dolphins and going snorkeling. Larry insisted that we take the

THE GIFT OF TODAY

trip because he couldn't guarantee he would feel better Thursday or Friday. And if the weather was worse, we wouldn't get to experience the adventure. He wanted to stay at the hotel and rest in the hot tub. After a few minutes of deliberation, I decided that Dina and I would take the catamaran trip.

We drove to Port Allen and caught the 8:15 catamaran. There were about 30 passengers plus a crew of four mates and the captain. This was a "barefoot cruise" so we had to give up our shoes. We had a choice of scuba diving or snorkeling so they knew which equipment to bring on board. Dina chose snorkeling. I chose neither. As we boarded the boat, I remembered almost being in tears and feeling guilty about the decision I had made. I prayed silently,

"*Lord, please keep us safe and don't let me get seasick on this boat. I will embarrass my daughter to death if I get ill. Please help me to hold it together. Please keep my husband safe and give him relief from his pain. Return us safely to my Larry because Lord, he doesn't even know where we are right now. Holy Spirit, be with us and guide me in my decisions. I pray these things in Jesus' name. Amen.*"

The crew was all quite friendly and we were served a continental breakfast. We were cruising along the west side of the island headed for the Na Pali Coast, which is quite calm in the summer months, but has a reputation for being unruly in the winter. We were experiencing some significant waves, and a few of the passengers who had been jumping on the trampoline that was on the front of the catamaran, had now taken seats. There were two people hanging over the edge of the boat vomiting, and I did my best not to look in their direction. That kind of thing can be contagious. Dina kept looking at me and asking if I was okay, to which I responded, "I'm fine." The truth was, I wanted to yell, "*Get me off this horrible boat and take me back to the island where my husband is!!*"

But, the weather was exquisite and except for the high waves, I was hanging in there very well. Dina seemed to be having a great time. She had her underwater camera with her and couldn't wait to snorkel and take photographs. About 9:30 a.m., as we moved around the west side of the island and began heading farther north, the Pacific Ocean began to change. The swell suddenly was between 20 to 25 feet and the boat was on one wild ride! Water came over the front of the boat in buckets and the Captain had to slow the boat considerably. I didn't like the look I saw on his face and I wanted to panic, but I knew I had to remain calm for my daughter's sake. We were all shuttled to a more secluded area in the back of the boat and told to get any of our belongings we had in the cabin underneath, as water was coming in. Dina ran down and got my purse. She had a very worried expression on her face when she returned, and I knew I looked frightened at that moment, because I WAS!!! We held onto each other and watched as at least ten people whose skin color had changed to putrid green, hung onto the sides of the boat and vomited into the ocean.

I was beginning to think the Captain had a death wish. And I was praying like I had never prayed before. I saw a look of fear in Dina's eyes and although she would probably never admit it, I knew that we both wondered if we would make it off that boat alive.

I mentally prepared myself to become part of the Pacific Ocean, although I had not yet said goodbye to my husband. It was at that moment that I remembered the Bible story about Jesus in the boat and how he asked his disciple Peter to walk to Him on the water. His disciple got out of the boat and began walking and a terrible wind came up. He immediately became afraid and did not trust God. I knew this was a test for me. I was determined that Dina and I would make it back to my husband at any cost, that I would trust God to calm these waters, and that I would make better judgments in the future. The waves continued for almost 20 minutes, when finally the Captain announced that we had a decision to make. He wanted us to vote as to whether we would continue north or turn around and find a different

THE GIFT OF TODAY

place to snorkel and dive. To my surprise, some of these people who were deathly sick voted to continue on. Thank God, clearer heads prevailed and the majority ruled to turn around. As soon as the boat changed direction, the waves calmed and the rest of the boat ride was incredible. We did get the opportunity to see whales twice –three humpbacks, then one adult and one baby. I took pictures and was actually quick enough to catch them on film. We saw several types of dolphins, and the "spinners" put on quite a show.

The diving instructors gave lessons to those passengers going scuba diving and snorkeling. We finally reached a spot that was calm and had interesting underwater caverns to explore. The divers got into all their gear and were helped over the side of the boat. About one-half of the passengers chose to dive, the other half to snorkel. I was the only passenger who stayed on board with the Captain. I was very proud of Dina for trying the snorkeling. At first it didn't appear that she was going to be able to do it. She kept swallowing water and losing her breath. Then all at once she relaxed with it, got the mouthpiece in her mouth correctly, and everything came together. She saw and took pictures of several different kinds of fish.

While we were anchored, another boat from their fleet was anchored in almost the exact same spot. The boats started floating toward each other until they were only inches apart. Our Captain ran to the back of the boat and pushed the other vessel as hard as he could with his foot, while the other Captain was steering to move the boat, and somehow managed to pass us without incident. I believe there was Divine Intervention on that one!! Good grief. I began to wonder just how experienced these people were, or if they were hitting the Mai Tai's before we came on board that morning!

Once everyone returned to the boat, lunch was served. We had sandwiches, fruit, salad, cookies, Mai Tai's, and any other type of drink, soft or hard, that we wanted. At that point, a Mai Tai was calling my name. It had been quite a morning. Before we knew it, we were back on shore and our six-hour adventure was history. *Praise the Lord*!

When we returned to the hotel, Larry was not in the room. We looked from the balcony and couldn't see him anywhere. About 30 minutes after we returned, he came back to the room looking well-rested and smiling, walking better than he had in days! He walked all over the hotel grounds, was in and out of the hot tub every ten minutes for two hours, and was doing fine. Amazing, considering what the day before was like. I was so thankful that it appeared his medicine was working again. He asked how our boat ride was, and Dina and I just told him that he had made the right decision for himself. He would have been very uncomfortable on that boat. I gave him a hug and didn't want to let go. I was so happy to see him and feel his arms around me again. I also hugged my beautiful daughter and was so thankful for her safety.

We weren't back an hour when Larry began complaining again about how bad his back was feeling. I couldn't believe it. And, he was hungry for.... McDonalds! Here we were in this beautiful place with incredible food all around us and he wanted McNuggets® and French fries. He and I took off in the car to a McDonalds three blocks from the hotel. As soon as he ate his dinner, he was grinning again from ear to ear. Just like a kid! I just didn't know what to think anymore.

We went to the lounge when we returned and joined Dina for a couple drinks and a few rounds of cards. There was Polynesian music and hula dancers in the open air bar and we enjoyed a beautiful evening. I gave Larry his medication before bed and asked if he would mind if I slept with Dina, to give him more room to move around in and make himself more comfortable. He thought that was a good idea. I hoped it would give him a better, more restful sleep. It appeared to have worked. We all slept in the following morning and didn't make it to the breakfast buffet until almost 10:00.

THE GIFT OF TODAY

Dina and I finished writing our post cards and considering that I hadn't planned to send any, I mailed fifteen. Dina and I went for a walk along the beach and Larry returned to the room to watch *Price Is Right*. Old habits die hard. We then got on with our day touring a different part of the island.

We headed north that day starting with the little town of Kapaa. It was a quaint little town with a fresh food market and a craft market of all items grown or made by hand on the island. Everything was surprisingly reasonable. We bought bananas, apple bananas, papaya, guava and homemade cookies. Larry and I walked, holding hands, down Main Street going in and out of shops. Dina found a surf shop she really liked. We left her there and continued walking back up the other side of the street towards the car. Thank God, that side of the street was in the shade. It was HOT!!! It was 85 degrees that day and the sun was just a scorcher.

Everyone on the island kept telling us how unseasonable the weather had been that week. Larry and I stopped at a street vendor who was selling flavored shaved ices, then sat on a park bench in the shade to wait for Dina.

Our next stop was the Guava Plantation in Kilauea, on the north coast of the island. There we sampled guava juice, jellies, jams and spreads mixed with other island fruits. Delicious! We also went into the plantation and picked our own fresh guavas to take back to the hotel.

From there, we headed farther north to the Kilauea Lighthouse. It sits on the northeast coast of the island. Behind it are huge cliffs where the water crashes and shoots hundreds of feet in the air. Occasionally, the roads on the north shore that are closest to the water are closed, with no through passage allowed. The beaches are closed almost all winter on the north shore.

Dianne Klancir

We continued north on Route 56 to the Hanalei Valley overlook. The fields at this overlook were growing taro, a plant used in the production of food on the island. The contrasting colors were lovely. There are many bridges along the north shore—several that are only one lane. There was one in particular that was slats of wood that looked badly in need of repair.

As we approached the community of Hanalei, we passed the Wai Oli Mission House (an Episcopal church) that was so quaint and darling I had to have a picture of it. Hanalei was a surfer's paradise. (It brought back memories of a song by Peter, Paul and Mary..."*Puff the Magic Dragon, lived by the sea, and frolicked in the autumn mist, in a land called Hanalei...*"©). The beaches were numerous and just the whole shopping and eating area looked like a surfer bum's delight. At this point, we were very close to the Wet Caves that Dina wanted to see. But the height of the waves left me wondering if the roads might be closed behind us if we proceeded any further. There was no other way back, so if they closed the roads we couldn't return to our hotel. Again, there was a difference of opinion because we would not risk going on.

On our return drive to Kapaa, Dina spotted waterfalls that were not identified on any of our maps, but were so beautiful, we stopped so she could take a picture. By this time, we were getting hungry. Larry had not complained of pain once that entire day, so we decided to forge on. We returned to the Fern Grotto where the open air restaurant overlooked the Wailua River. We had no idea we would be entertained by water skiers on the river during our meal. It was like "dinner and a show".

When we returned to the hotel, Larry grimaced again in pain. I gave him his medication and settled him into bed. Again, I let him have the entire bed in order to have his best nights sleep.

Dina and I went down to the lounge to listen to some music and talk. She had talked to Adam earlier, who said he would buy Larry a

THE GIFT OF TODAY

birthday cake for the day we returned home from our trip so that we could have a little party for him. We were returning right on Larry's birthday, even though his celebration had been three months before. It was a very sweet and thoughtful thing to do. Dina had spoken to Adam at least once every day and even though we had taken her to Paradise for Christmas, her heart was with Adam. I knew she couldn't wait to return home to see him.

Unfortunately, Larry couldn't sleep and walked the floors all night. I gave him more medication and rubbed his back, but it gave him little comfort. I began to wonder what we were going to do if this pain didn't subside.

How were we going to get him home? Those two flights were long and if there was turbulence, he would be in agony. I prayed and cried and begged for mercy for my husband. I again asked for wisdom to know the right thing to do.

After breakfast in our room, we decided that it was a good day to relax and enjoy the beach. (I didn't have the heart to ask Larry to sit in the car another day.) Dina and Larry jumped into their swimsuits and I went down to the beach in my shorts. He climbed into the hot tub and looked like he had stepped into Heaven. That must have felt so good to him. He would stay in ten minutes and then get out ten minutes, and he continued that for over two hours again.

After lunch, Dina and I went back into Kapaa, just a few minutes away, for a Kauai Products Fair. We bought coconut-scented lotion made locally, seashells, and some photographs professionally taken on the island. Everything there was very inexpensive. It was a great place to shop.

When we returned to the hotel, Larry helped us pack all our souvenirs into the corrugated box I had found and seal it up for shipment. I didn't think they would let us take all that on the plane so we decided to ship it home. It took about a week to arrive, and if I would have realized that other people had far more than we did and brought it on the plane, I would have saved the expense of sending it and insuring its safe arrival.

By dinner time, Larry felt up to a short ride. We went about five minutes away to a Thai restaurant called Mema's. Then we walked around the corner for some frozen yogurt. There had not been a bad weather day on Kauai since our arrival. There were thunderstorms one evening on the north side of the island, but we were unaffected by it.

The next day we caught up on the sights we had missed thus far. We visited some beautiful temples and a graveyard. I had never seen anything so beautifully maintained. The lawn looked manicured and the flowers were fabulous—so many varieties that we had never seen before, and one more lavish than the other. We did a little more souvenir shopping and went to the post office to mail our souvenirs. Larry began having terrible back pain and spasms. We hustled him back to the hotel so he could lay down.

I spent the rest of the afternoon trying to reach our medical doctor on the mainland to ask what we should do. He suggested doubling all his medications (pain and anti-inflammatories) until we got back and then come into the doctor's office the morning after we returned.

I gave Larry his double dose of pills and he wanted to go down to the hot tub. We went down with him and visited with other vacationers who were also enjoying the water. When Larry was in that hot tub, he seemed the most relaxed. That water must have felt so wonderful. When he was done, we had our last dinner at the hotel. He stayed at the table long enough to eat his meal and then excused himself to the room. We found him lying on his side watching TV when we returned. He just couldn't get comfortable. That night he tossed and turned and was awake most of the night. He said he was nervous about the return flight home wondering what he was going to do if he was in pain on the airplane. I explained again what the doctor advised me to do, and reassured him that everything would be alright. He just didn't appear to be buying it.

It was sad leaving Kauai. It was such a tremendous place. Larry

THE GIFT OF TODAY

asked me if I thought I could live there and I told him no. I liked having things close by when I wanted them. I didn't want to have to travel from island to island to make a major purchase, such as furniture, appliances, etc., and have to pay all the shipping charges that go along with it. But it sure was a great place to visit!

We boarded the plane to return home on December 30, Larry's 75th birthday (at last), and it was another magnificent day on the island. Tail winds blew us into L.A. much sooner than we were expected. That was good news because Larry was starting to get uncomfortable in his seat. When we landed, he was able to stretch his legs again and he needed that.

Soon we were back up in the air and on our way to Chicago. Larry slept part of the way back, which was good. The double doses of medicine were doing the job and he looked fairly comfortable. But then again, the poor guy was exhausted from not sleeping the night before.

We arrived in Chicago earlier than expected also, but Adam was ready for us—or, should I say, Dina! He met us in the baggage claim area and it was like a scene from a love story in slow motion. He held his arms open and as she ran to meet him, they just seemed to melt into each other. They were so happy to be in each other's arms again.

Larry fell asleep as soon as we pulled out of the airport parking lot and slept in my arms most of the way home. He didn't realize that when we arrived home there would be a little birthday celebration for him. Adam had picked up a decorated cake and ice cream and had everything prepared for a birthday party when we walked in the door. Our dog, Molly, practically knocked Larry over when he walked in the house. She was so excited to see him. Naturally, we all got our share of excitement from her but Larry was always Molly's favorite. She might have been my gift from Larry, but she was definitely Larry's dog. They had a very special bond.

Larry was so surprised to have another little party and he expressed how thoughtful Adam was to do that. After our little celebration, Larry settled in front of the fireplace. It was a typical cold, windy, Midwestern winter day. It wasn't long and he was fast asleep. Dina, Adam and I talked about the trip and what beautiful memories we would always have of Kauai and our Christmas there. We knew that Larry enjoyed it as much as he possibly could, but in the back of my mind, I wondered if he had been given the option of backing out of that trip if he would have stayed home. I believed he went because he knew how much it meant to Dina and me to be in such a special place, as a family, for Christmas.

I began to unpack and settle back into reality. It actually felt good to be back in our own home, our own beds. Tomorrow would be spent in the doctor's office to find out what this nagging back pain was from, and hopefully give my husband some relief. I helped Larry up into our bed and prayed that God would look with favor on us and bless Larry with some answers and comfort. I thanked Him for safe travel, beautiful weather and doctors that understood our plight and came to our rescue. I thanked Him for my husband's courage and faith and I wondered in silence if I were in his position if I would have braved this trip. I also thanked Him for allowing our family to experience Christmas together in Kauai. *Praise God from whom all blessings flow.*

CHAPTER SEVENTEEN

Livin' In The Valley

The following day I called the doctor whom we had contacted from Hawaii about Larry's back pain. He wanted Larry in his office immediately for x-rays of his ribs. The x-rays showed old fractures he had received the night of Dina's post-prom, when we were decorating the gym and he fell off the scaffolding and landed on the bleachers.

I will never forget how scared I was that night, as I watched him fall. He was determined not to let anything ruin all the plans we had made for those kids on prom night, so he refused to stop working, refused to go to the doctor, and insisted that I pressure wrap an ice pack around the area so he could continue what he was doing. I cried the entire time I wrapped it because he would wince in pain. He had incredible pain tolerance. We found out later, he had cracked three ribs.

Larry had insisted on driving to the doctor's appointment the Monday after we returned from Kauai. Rather than argue with him, I let him drive. On the way, we spotted a deer on the side of the road. Rather than slow down, he continued on at the same speed ,and the deer ran in front of our car. Larry didn't even make an attempt to slow down or swerve. There was actually plenty of time to react, and he just seemed to slam right into it. Neither of us was hurt, and it didn't put our car out of commission at all, it just needed about $2,000 in repair. I began to sense some confusion in Larry that day and watched it closely. *Is this old age? He's 75. Or, in some way, is the stress of fighting cancer and back pain taking a toll on his faculties?* Regardless of the cause, from that point on, he let me do the driving.

The doctor prescribed muscle relaxants and a stronger pain medication. We tried that for a couple days, and there seemed to be little improvement. The pain kept radiating down his legs and he couldn't lay or sit without being in some pain, and his back kept popping out of place. He couldn't cough, he couldn't sleep, he was just miserable. I was beside myself. I decided to call the oncologist and let her know what was happening. She was not happy with me that I consulted with an M.D. instead of her. I tried to explain that when the diagnosis was not "bone cancer" but rather "severe arthritis," it seemed more appropriate to seek help from the M.D. She did not agree. She wanted to see him immediately.

Fortunately, I was able to get him into the car. It was getting too painful for him to ride in a vehicle. The oncologist took the medications away that the M.D. had prescribed and gave him Dilaudid®, a very strong narcotic medication. She also gave him a med to help coat his stomach and another one to help with the constipation he was sure to have from the narcotic. She basically gave us free reign with the Dilaudid®, but said to try to limit it to every three to four hours. I gave him a dose as soon as we got home and another before bed that night. By the next day, he was feeling slightly better and I actually observed smiles from him. He made it to church that weekend and was able to sit through the entire service. Naturally, as soon as he was feeling better he wanted to return to work, but the oncologist said he needed more time.

That Tuesday, Larry had an MRI of his spine. His friend Earl drove him to the hospital for the MRI so that I could go to work. He was

THE GIFT OF TODAY

feeling fairly comfortable after a few days of continuous Dilaudid®, and they had an enjoyable ride together. Earl really pampered Larry, and I was so grateful to him for his grace under pressure.

The following morning the oncologist asked us to get his test results in person. That didn't sound good to me. I figured if there was any way she could have spared us another 45-minute drive in the car each way to an appointment, she would have. I braced myself. God truly held us both in the palm of His hand and had taken good care of us. There were times my strength was zapped, but knowing we weren't going through this alone, put it all into perspective. It wasn't ME seeing us through this ordeal.

So, on Wednesday morning, Larry and I found ourselves in the oncologist's office, hoping for the best, but expecting the worst. The MRI showed that the thoracic and lumbar spine was loaded with arthritis, spurs, and disc disease. He had stenosis (narrowing) of the upper thoracic area and there was stenosis and severe arthritis in the lower lumbar spine. In addition, the MRI showed a TUMOR (*there's that "T" word again*), about two to two-and-a-half centimeters in the soft tissue around the spinal cord. He was given a larger dose of Dilaudid®, another med for his stomach and an anti-inflammatory. This concerned me because I had been seeing increased confusion in Larry since being on the Dilaudid®. He was also going to need ten radiation treatments to his spine as soon as possible.

I remember grabbing Larry's hand, looking down at the floor and saying out loud "God grant me the serenity to accept the things I cannot change, the courage to change the things I can, and the wisdom to know the difference."©

I wanted to scream out loud and never stop! There was absolutely nothing I could change about any of this. It was totally out of my control and I hated that. I could only be there for support and advocacy and I did both to the best of my ability.

Dianne Klancir

Larry's oncologist looked him in the eye and said, "I am so sorry. But let's attack this with a vengeance. I'll call the radiologist and tell her you are on the way over to be measured and start your treatments." We began the long walk over to the Radiation Department.

As we began our shuffle, hand-in-hand, over to Radiology, I recalled a poem.

Sometimes life seems hard to bear,
full of sorrow, trouble and woe.
It's then I have to remember,
that it's in the valleys I grow.

If I always stayed on the mountain top
and never experienced pain,
I would never appreciate God's love
and would be living in vain.

I have so much to learn
and my growth is very slow,
Sometimes I need the mountain tops
but it's in the valleys I grow.

I do not always understand
why things happen as they do,
But I am very sure of one thing,
my Lord will see me through.

My little valleys are nothing
when I picture Christ on the cross.
He went through the valley of death,
His victory was Satan's loss.

THE GIFT OF TODAY

Forgive me Lord, for complaining
when I'm feeling so very low.
Just give me a gentle reminder
that it's in the valleys I grow.

Continue to strengthen me, Lord,
and use my life each day,
To show your love to others
and help them find their way.

Thank you for the valleys, Lord,
for this one thing I know.
The mountain tops are glorious,
but it's in the valleys I grow.

By Jane Eggleston

There were so many times in our lives that Larry and I felt like we were on top of the world. I know we took so many opportunities for granted. We spent money foolishly, we were selfish with our time, and we didn't take the time to praise God regularly for everything we had been so generously given. I wondered if this was supposed to be a growing time, an awakening for us, because we were certainly in the valley now. Larry was physically the weakest he had ever been in his life, and I was totally surrendered to God for answers. I found myself having a relationship with the Holy Spirit over these past few months that I had never had before. I kept asking myself if I had to be brought to my knees in order for me to realize I was not in control of my destiny or anyone else's. There was a much greater power that was calling the shots here and I needed to pay close attention.

Dianne Klancir

The radiologist met with us again. (*Yep, it's us!*) And, after taking the measurements they needed, he had the first treatment immediately. He needed to return every day for nine weekdays. There were no treatments on weekends. He handled it so well. I believe he was quietly resolved to do whatever God wanted him to do. We were both feeling very led by the Spirit. I was very hopeful that once the tumor had shrunk somewhat that we would be able to reduce some of these strong pain medications he was taking to alleviate some of his confusion.

He said that evening that he felt better than he had in weeks. What a shame we couldn't have done this for him before our trip so he could have enjoyed it more. It was too hard to look back and say "what if." So we just told ourselves that this was a learning experience and we would be smarter the next time.

I wanted to believe in my heart that one treatment gave him that much relief. *If that were the case, what would ten treatments do for him?* We could only wait and see. God's grace and mercy were sufficient for me and He was showering us with it every day. We were so blessed.

The following day, Larry started out with breakfast and his fistful of pills and we headed to the hospital for his second radiation treatment. As we neared the hospital, I noticed that Larry seemed slumped over and his color was an odd shade of green. I pulled into the parking lot and ran around to his door. As soon as I opened it, he took a deep breath and the color started to return to his face. He stepped out of the car and took another deep breath. He said he had never been so nauseated in his life. I waited until he felt he could proceed, and we walked arm in arm to the door of the hospital. I flagged down a volunteer for a wheelchair, but in typical Larry fashion, he would not ride in it. "I'm not ready for that yet," he scolded.

The radiation oncologist added an anti-nausea drug to the mix so that he could have the benefit of the other drugs without getting sick. It was incredible. We had to tell ourselves that the benefits of all this medicine outweighed the risks, and they did.

THE GIFT OF TODAY

The Radiation Department nursing staff was always warm and welcoming. He actually enjoyed going there to see them, but the treatments were wearing him to a frazzle. He didn't have the desire to do much when he came home except curl up in front of the fireplace and nap. That was fine. At least he didn't seem to be in pain. But what a difference from the last time he went through radiation. The location of these treatments was much harder on him.

The following day I returned to work and a friend of ours, Alan, took Larry to his radiation appointment. Larry was feeling strong and we were so grateful that Alan had volunteered to take him to a two-minute treatment so that I could go into work for a day.

Alan dropped Larry off at my place of employment after his appointment, and he spent the afternoon in my office. I didn't want to leave him home alone because of his confusion. He was having difficulty finding the right words and seemed a little disoriented. But, he also seemed to sense that he shouldn't be left alone.

I hoped that at some point, with the tumor shrinking, we could back off on some of these pills. I knew he was feeling somewhat better because he was begging for snow so that he could use the new tractor/snow thrower he had purchased. The new Sears 21 horsepower was "itching to be driven" as Larry put it. I, on the other hand, was praying that the weather remained stable throughout his treatments and the long rides to and from the hospital. He was in no condition to drive a moving vehicle anyway, even if it was just a lawn tractor. I figured when God thought Larry was ready to use the snow blower, he would provide enough snow for him.

That evening, he asked to cut back on his pain medicine because he was feeling pain-free. The inflammation had apparently decreased, so he continued everything else, except I also cut back his steroid dose. I thought the steroids might be making him nauseated. When I informed the oncologist a couple days later about what I had done, she told me he HAD to have the higher level of steroid and that it was the location of the radiation treatments that was making him nauseous, not the pills. *Live and learn.* She then gave us two more medications to help with his stomach discomfort and nausea. These were scripts number nine and ten we had filled since returning home from Kauai. Naturally, as a nurse, I wanted my husband to be pain-free and taking whatever medicines would benefit him, but I also knew the side effects of some of these drugs, and combining some of them was frightening.

Over the weekend, Dina came home and we shared photos of our trip. She was so grateful to see her dad looking more comfortable than the last time she'd seen him. They had a wonderful visit together.

By the end of the weekend, Larry had been two days without a radiation treatment and had barely taken pain medication. His confusion had decreased, I realized, because there was a telephone call while I was in the shower and he actually remembered who it was! That was a tremendous improvement.

We even watched the Green Bay Packers play football on Sunday, which was a treat for me and a painful experience for Larry, Mr. Chicago Bear! Other than going to church that morning, he had not been out of the house, so I treated him to dinner at a nearby restaurant. He seemed relieved to get out of the house a bit, and I noticed his appetite seemed back to normal. I was thankful for that, because he needed three good-sized meals each day with all the medication he was taking.

Monday, January 14, 2002, was an expensive day. Our two-year old washing machine died an unnatural—and post warranty—death, so we had to buy a new one. It was also the day I had to have our car repaired from the deer accident. On the way home with the loaner car, nine deer ran in front of me. Fortunately, there was no collision.

Marilyn, one of Larry's relatives, drove him to radiation treatment number four. I didn't realize that on Mondays the radiation oncolo-

THE GIFT OF TODAY

gist also visited with him, or I would have accompanied him to that treatment. He had done so well over the weekend, I figured he should be able to go to this quickie treatment with Marilyn and I would see him at home in the afternoon. The radiation oncologist began talking with him and as she asked him questions and heard him try to muddle his way through the answers, it became apparent to her that he was very confused. (She hadn't realized how confused he was the week before because I answered most of her questions at that appointment. He was better by this time. A whole lot better). She decided that he needed another CAT scan of the brain and left lung.

Yes, she believed the cancer had spread even further and his confusion wasn't just from his meds, but from metastases to the brain. I saw this coming but still wanted to believe that once we decreased or discontinued some of his medication this would all go away. Oh, how I wanted to believe that. I was hanging on to hope by a thread.

It stood to reason that if the cancer had spread to his pleural fluid and his spinal cord that it was in his spinal fluid too. The next logical site would be the brain—*if there is any logic in cancer.* He would have that test in two days. I prayed that he wouldn't try to escape from the house, fall down the stairs, eat something that could hurt him or take pills when I wasn't looking. I felt like the warden in a high-security prison.

Marilyn picked Larry up the next day for his radiation treatment, and on the way home they were to stop at the medical doctor's clinic nearby to have some blood work drawn. That was all being done locally. When they pulled into the parking lot, Larry stepped out of the car and vomited. Marilyn assisted him into the building and he raced for the restroom to continue what he had started outside.

That night after dinner, he vomited his meal. This was not going well. He hadn't told me before dinner that he still felt sick or I would have made a much more bland dinner. We changed his diet to 7-up, dry crackers and Jello®.

Dianne Klancir

In the pit of my stomach, I had a sickening feeling I had not felt before. I started to believe that this wasn't going to get better and I could feel my insides tremoring. I didn't want to see my husband suffer. He was always the epitome of strength and good health. He hadn't had a sick day from work in the 25 years he worked in the Chicago suburbs. His only sick time since moving here was when he had been diagnosed with cancer.

I thought about how much I loved the strength and size of his hands – the hands that caressed me when we made love or when I was scared. The hands that held our daughter in the hospital when she was born and made her feel secure with him from her first day. The hard-working hands that were sometimes rough from the labor-intensive work Larry did, both on his job and at home. The hands that made beautiful woodworking projects that people still treasure. The hands that reached out to the elderly at the nursing home and offered assistance. The hand that bore his wedding ring that said we were one until eternity. I loved those hands. As I looked at them now, they looked old and frail. They were still beautiful hands, but they were wasting away.

I asked God to be merciful and if the cancer had spread to the brain, that God would take him quickly. I couldn't believe I had uttered those words. My prayers had definitely changed. It was a turning point for me. I didn't want to just chase this cancer around his body and lose him one piece at a time. He was too good a man to have that happen and I couldn't bear to see him suffer. I was exhausted and I couldn't imagine how he felt. He had been through so much and just kept marching on, looking forward and expecting the best—we both did. I prepared myself for the fact that we could be facing his mortality here. It finally began to sink in. As a nurse, I helped people make life and death decisions over the years, but it was different now that it was my spouse. This was the man I loved, my best friend. I admired his

THE GIFT OF TODAY

strength so much and so did many others. He was a trooper. I knew I could not have held up as well under the same circumstances. *Lord, I begged, have mercy.*

So, it was back up to the hospital for the CAT scans of the lung and brain and his next radiation treatment for his back. The results of the CAT scans would not be in until the following day. That was the longest night of my life. I tried not to think about it. I tried to focus on spending quality time with Larry and doing things we enjoyed, and to smile and pretend everything was okay, but in the back of my mind, I knew. I just knew.

The next day, we were summoned to the hospital radiation department for the test results before they did his treatment. I was shaking badly but didn't want Larry to see that. He almost looked oblivious that day as to what was going on around him.

The radiation oncologist entered the room and held Larry's hand. "I have good news and bad news, Larry."

"Okay", he said, "Give me the good news first just in case something happens to me in the next few minutes." She smiled at that.

The good news was that the lung scan showed that the tumor was still virtually so tiny they could barely see it. The bad news was that the brain scan showed four tumors that weren't there last April. Three tumors were on one side of the brain and they were about the size of marbles; the one on the other side was the size of a golf ball.

I began to shake from head to toe. I felt like I had been hit in the gut with brass knuckles. I actually had to keep myself from throwing up. *How could this be? He had done so well.* I hated cancer and felt anger at this disease. I wanted to yell at somebody and scream until I had no voice left. My worst nightmares were becoming reality. It just didn't seem possible. It was like an out-of-body experience. We had been living on the mountain top. Our lives were filled with simple pleasures, family, fun, travel, and friends. We didn't have things go wrong like this. We were unmistakably in the valley now. I know the radiologist kept talking to Larry, but I never heard a word after that. I sobbed aloud and just stared ahead. I could feel Larry's hands squeezing mine at the moment when she gave us the news, and then I felt them lose their grip as she described the tumors. I began feeling him pull away and it scared the hell out of me.

I couldn't lose Larry. I felt he was my rock, my strength. I had become so dependent on him over the years that I didn't know how I could exist without him. I had been such an independent person before I met Larry but all that had changed. He would always say that he found out about my "battles" after they had already been fought. But, I knew that if I had told him about issues I was dealing with at work or wherever, he would have tried to come to my rescue. He always wanted to be my knight in shining armor. I just wanted him to be there to listen and understand, and he did that, but he always wanted to fix everything for me and make it better. I could bounce anything off him and know that he would tell me what I NEEDED to hear, not just what I WANTED to hear.

Take a deep breath, Dianne. Breathe in, breathe out. Then call Dina and give her this news.

Good Lord, how strong do you think I am???

CHAPTER EIGHTEEN

"Am I Glowing Yet??"

It was the most heart-wrenching experience in the world breaking the news to my daughter, that her father's cancer had again spread to a new location. The words stuck in my throat and I held back tears as best I could. But, I just could not keep from crying when I heard Dina sobbing over the phone.

"I'll be home for the weekend," she cried. "Maybe I should take time off and just stay with you guys."

"Let's just see how the weekend plays out and not do that yet. I may need that from you later. But thank you for wanting to be here."

I wished I could've held her close instead of hanging up the phone and leaving her in Madison to deal with this. It was an absolutely awful thing to do to her. I felt so guilty. But, I would have felt guiltier had she found out from someone other than me. There were so many times I wanted to be selfish and say, "Please stay here and don't go back home. I need you here." And, I know she would have stayed. But, it wouldn't have been fair to her to lose her job, her apartment, and everything she had worked so hard for.

The next day it was time to pack up the car again and head for the Radiology Department of the hospital. There, we would begin the process of radiation to a new site and continue the treatments to his back that were already in progress. I remember thinking how strange the position was that he was required to lay in to get the correct angle for each treatment.

They made him a mask out of some type of silicone, and prepared him for the treatment to his head. The radiation oncologist explained everything well. Larry was now getting treatment number seven to his back and number one to his head. The doctor warned that his scalp may get quite sore and that he would probably lose his hair again. Larry had kept a buzz cut anyway, so he just shrugged when she told him that.

"Hey, I'm gonna have Yul (Brenner) back again!" I said excitedly. Larry just rolled his eyes. The biggest question for me was if this would clear up his confusion or if that was related to his medications. If it was caused by medication, would we have to cope with continued confusion AND the effects from radiation to two sites, all at the same time? *Lord, give me strength.*

We gave each other a long kiss when they called him into the treatment room. Tears were streaming down my face. Larry wiped them away with his hand and said, "No time for tears. Let's get this show on the road," and patted me on the behind as he walked away. Unbelievable. I turned around to see an elderly couple sitting there, watching us and waiting their turn. They were crying and laughing at the same time. Larry had such a good outlook on everything and he was so physically strong, it amazed me. The doctors and nurses loved him. He responded to treatment so well and did whatever he was told.

It's difficult to explain what an emotional roller coaster this was. Just when we thought we were past the worst and going to beat this, it showed up in another place that was inoperable, and we started all over again. Larry's strength and faith were unwavering. I could not have endured what he did.

THE GIFT OF TODAY

I prayed while I waited for his treatments to be completed. Soon he exited the radiation area with this big smile on his face and said to me, "Am I glowing yet?" I just slapped my forehead with my hand and shook my head. *How could somebody go through two radiation treatments to his back and brain and be in good humor?* It was beyond me.

We returned for another treatment the next day, and I actually thought I saw his confusion and word finding improve after just those two treatments. It was a prayer answered again.

Dina came home for the weekend to spend time with her dad. They played air hockey, she cooked for him, they went for a walk and we went to church together. It was so nice to have quality time together as a family in the comfort of our own home. Dina could find so many ways to make her dad smile. She knew the right things to say and teased him endlessly. She talked about her relationship with Adam that appeared to be getting more serious. Adam joined us for part of the weekend. Larry always enjoyed having him there because he didn't feel so "outnumbered" when there was another guy in the house. He would say, "Even the dog in this house is female. A poor guy doesn't stand a chance."

The weekend was actually very comfortable for Larry. The pain in his back had subsided after eight treatments, which meant that he could cut back on pain medication. That helped reduce the nausea that still occurred following treatments. Reducing medication made him more alert and he wasn't nauseous the entire weekend. (Taking two anti-nausea pills as soon as he got out of bed each morning really did the trick.) He had not used the shorter-acting pain pills in four days, so basically he was only taking NSAIDS and steroids. The plan was to reduce those as soon as he could tolerate it. Things were looking quite positive.

Late afternoon Sunday we went out for Chinese food with Adam, Dina, and Adam's dad and step-mom. It was the first time we had all shared a meal, and it was very pleasant. Larry didn't join in the conversation a lot because he still occasionally struggled to find the right words. But, he enjoyed the conversation and laughter and that was always good for him.

When we got home, we dragged out Dina's baby pictures and reminisced through stacks of albums. Adam was interested in learning all about Dina in her younger years and we laughed a lot. It was so cathartic for all of us. We also looked at our wedding album pictures and reminisced about that day.

Larry and I were married on July 4th, 1976. It was the year of the Bi-centennial and we chose that day because the hall where we wanted our reception was available. The next date they had open was the following January. We hemmed and hawed about what to do. The owner of the hall agreed to throw in the most marvelous wedding cake we could find and unlimited champagne if we booked that date. It was too good to pass up.

The minister had been in a parade that day and wore a traditional costume on the float, so we asked him to wear it for our ceremony. He was dressed in black knickers, a black cape, a three-pointed hat, and a ruffled shirt. Our wedding guests roared when he walked into the church. It was so much fun. The guys wore white tux jackets and blue pants and had a red, white and blue ruffle down their shirts (typical 70's stuff). The girls wore red dresses with navy bodices and short red over jackets trimmed in white. It was quite festive.

When we exited the church, firecrackers were set off rather than throwing rice. Our cake had miniature firecrackers on it and was the most unique wedding cake I had ever seen. They took it apart in layers. It was so large the waitresses had to climb ladders to disassemble it. We had an elegant sit-down dinner and Larry and I stayed until the

THE GIFT OF TODAY

very end of the party. We didn't want to miss a moment. Ah, what great memories.

Larry, Dina, Adam and I played cards until the wee hours of the morning. Since Monday was a holiday, none of us had to get up for work. But, Larry had to be at his next radiation treatments. Thankfully, Tuesday would be the last treatment to his back. Then we could concentrate totally on what was going on in the brain.

While Larry was in radiation that Monday, his son Les had prostate surgery. His wife Judy called to tell us that everything went well and they believed they had removed all the cancer. That was the news Larry wanted to hear about his son.

On Tuesday I returned to work for the first time in almost a week. Our friends Dave and Eleanor took Larry to his final back treatment and fourth treatment to the brain. Later, his friend Richard (who is a minister) stopped by the house to visit. They were golf partners in tournaments and always had a lot of laughs together. My sister Margie and her husband also visited us that evening. We appreciated so much when people took the time to think about us and pay a visit. I've heard people say that sometimes when a serious illness sets in, friends shy away because they don't know what to say or do. They don't want to interfere or feel like they are imposing, but they want to be supportive. We were so fortunate that our friends seemed to rally around and be there for us whenever we needed them most. It was especially nice when his male friends came around, and it wasn't just the women who were expressing their friendship. That means a lot to a male patient.

Larry's confusion seemed to be improving, except for the word finding. At least the thought processes seemed to be a little better. Maybe I was just being optimistic. I had to hang onto something.

Larry lost three pounds in one week. That was the single largest weight loss since the very early stages of his diagnosis when he had literally just stopped eating. I brought home a Kentucky Fried Chicken® dinner that evening, to entice him to eat. Not the healthiest food in the world, but the poor guy had been eating healthy for a long time and hadn't been able to enjoy anything he really craved. His eyes danced and he ate every crumb! He was moving around like a kid again and said his back pain was gone. Incredible.

Judy called to update us on Les's condition. The night after surgery had been difficult. There was still a great deal of swelling and drainage today, but the seriousness of the previous night seemed to have passed. Larry was so relieved.

After treatment number five, Larry had enough energy to unload the dishwasher and fold a load of laundry. I was shocked! He still had difficulty speaking at times, but his thoughts were tracking and it was heartwarming to see. I told him how grateful I was for his help and explained that he wasn't expected to do those things.

"You have done so much for me, that this is the only way I have to repay you," he said.

"Larry, that's what wives do for their husbands. Remember those vows? In sickness and in health.... This is what wives do."

"Not all wives!" he retorted. "I'm a lucky guy." He hugged me and it felt so good to feel his strength around me. I loved when he held me in his arms. It was the most comforting feeling.

"I'm the lucky one," I said. "I haven't been an easy person to live with and you have stuck by me through every decision, every crisis, everything. I love you for that."

"That's what husbands do," he laughed.

"Not all husbands!" We melted into each other's arms again and he kissed me passionately. I thanked God for bringing this man into my life. I knew that each time I wept over Larry that God was weeping with me. I knew He felt my pain and He was there with me every step of the way. I felt His presence at all times.

THE GIFT OF TODAY

Late Thursday evening Adam arrived to take Larry to his Friday morning radiation treatment (number seven). Larry was doing a little better each day and so each day brought another med reduction of one type or another. Adam had been to school that day and worked all evening, then drove to our house from Aurora. I could tell that he didn't sleep well that night, because he was already up and dressed when we awoke. Larry insisted on making them both breakfast and he seemed to be able to handle it, so I went to work.

Adam drove Larry to his treatment and then they bowled two games together. They went to lunch and then to visit some of Larry's co-workers at the nursing home. Adam drove all the way back to Aurora to work, and following work, drove to Madison to visit Dina. I asked God to keep him awake and alert on the roads so that he didn't hurt himself or someone else with as little sleep as he had.

Much to my surprise, Larry asked me that evening if we could go to Las Vegas and Arizona at Easter break. I almost fell off my chair. Then he really lowered a bombshell on me. Twenty-six years ago, when we met, I was a snow-skier and wanted Larry to learn. He refused, saying he was afraid he might fall and break a bone. Out of the clear blue, now he wanted to snow ski! So, Dina, who had become an excellent skier, was going to take her dad when we had our next big snowfall. I just shook my head in disbelief. I told him that was fine as long as we got the doctor's release before he did that, but I wondered what in the world he would come up with next!

After lunching with friends on Saturday, we stopped at the Fannie May candy store. This was Larry's last week of radiation and he wanted to bring the staff a treat—a three-and-a-half pound box of chocolate! We left it in the car, because the temptation of that much Fannie May in my house was too much to bear.

The following day Larry and I were greeters at church and everyone made a big fuss over him, which he loved. He was really the center of attention, and seemed to enjoy it.

Monday, I accompanied Larry to treatment number eight. The doctor was pleased with the way he looked physically, but he had lost eight pounds this week. That was huge. He was eating smaller meals and I was filling in with liquid supplements in between, but that was still a large weight loss. He gave the staff their candy, and one by one they gave him a kiss and hug. He ate that right up. *If only that could have put pounds on him!!*

I noticed that Larry's behavior toward me was changing. I really felt like he was pushing me away at times. He would get very short with me and then seemed to have no recollection of the event later. He was pleasant enough with everyone else, so I thought maybe it was because I had gotten too overbearing. Sometimes the person closest to the patient catches the brunt of their anger in these situations. He really hadn't expressed anything like that before now.

Tuesday, his cousin Joe took him for treatment number nine. They hadn't seen each other for quite awhile, so there was a lot of catching up to do. Larry was so pleased when he found out a couple years prior that Joe was his "long lost relative."

The following day our friend Bob was taking Larry for his last appointment, and I prayed that the weather would hold up. The reports said that the snow would start sometime in the afternoon, and we had been so fortunate throughout all these treatments. We just needed one more day. They were predicting we could get as much as twelve inches. I guess we knew the day would come that we would finally get our winter weather.

Larry was back home on Wednesday by 2:00 p.m. and the snow started shortly after that. That was his final radiation appointment and he would have to return in one month for a CT scan to see how the tumors were affected by the treatments. The staff in the Radiation

THE GIFT OF TODAY

Department had thrown a little party for him with hats, party favors, noise makers, and they took a picture together. Had I known that was going to happen, I would have taken the day off and taken him to that appointment. He was less than kind that night as he let me know that I should have been there with him. I felt guilty enough and didn't need that extra dose. I called the doctor and mentioned the personality changes in the past few days. She thought it would improve once he was weaned off the steroids. I hoped she was right.

On Thursday morning at 5:00 a.m., my employer called to tell me to stay home because of the severe weather. What a great place to work! We looked out the window and couldn't believe our eyes. We had our first real winter blizzard. It was our first day of no radiation, no treatments of any kind, no commitments to rush off to. We went back to sleep. It was awesome.

We had ten inches of snow that morning and Larry suited up to go out and snow blow. As he opened the garage door, he realized the neighbors had already blown the snow out of our driveway for us. He was appreciative and disappointed at the same time. He had waited forever it seemed, to use that new toy he had gotten. I reassured him that this would not be our last snowfall. By late afternoon, between the sun, the city plows and the salt they applied, the streets were clear and we went out. I drove Larry to McDonalds® for a strawberry shake and we went coffee klatching. Larry had a few testy moments but for the most part appeared happy that I had the day off with him. I was glad that he had not remembered the promise he and Dina made each other about going skiing. I just couldn't see him trying that at this stage of the game, and it would have meant a drive to Madison to meet up with her.

On Friday, we BOTH returned to work. Larry hadn't been to work in quite some time, and decided that with the doctor's approval, he wanted to try it. It was actually a very special treat for him, because the Maintenance Department was serving pancake breakfast to all the employees that day, and they wanted him there to help cook. Let me tell you, that was the best medicine we could have given Larry. He was so excited to be asked to do that. When he got home in the early afternoon, he literally crashed. He was exhausted. Dina stopped over for supper on her way to Aurora to see Adam for the weekend and brought along a pan of her scrumptious spinach lasagna so that I didn't have to cook. She cleaned up the kitchen before she left and vowed to return on Sunday on her way back to Madison. "Love 'ya dad. Hang tough," she would say as she hugged him goodbye. "Be safe" were always her final instructions.

On Saturday, we drove into the Chicago suburbs to visit Larry's son, Les, who was at home recuperating. We wouldn't stay long because we never knew what the weather would bring in January, but Larry needed to see and hug his son. It was good for both of them. His son and family had a much better attitude than the last time we had seen them and seemed grateful for our visit.

I always wished that Larry and his kids would have had a closer relationship but I guess that with second marriages that happens sometimes. At least Larry and this son had kept in touch.

I kept playing over and over in my mind just how blessed we had been. Larry had twenty radiation treatments in January, which is usually the worst winter month in the Midwest. But, there had been no snow from the time he started until he finished. Larry was home exactly twenty-five minutes when the snow started falling and we got dumped on. Our friends gathered around and took turns taking Larry to treatments so I could continue working and it gave Larry someone other than me to talk with. God was good all the time, and all the time, God was good.

THE GIFT OF TODAY

"Heavenly Father, we are so humbled by your presence in our lives. We know that we are so lucky to know you and be able to talk with you. We can feel you with us every step on this journey, and we feel your tears as we shed ours. You are an awesome God who gives us the strength we need and you feed us with your Word to keep us faithful. Lord, we ask you to bless our friends and family who have responded to our needs and we ask you to keep them safe and healthy. We thank you for a wonderful daughter and for Adam who has been a great source of strength for Dina. We thank you for unbelievable employers who realize the importance of family and have put no pressure on us. Lord, we ask that you continue to watch over us and keep us safe. In Jesus' precious name, we pray. Amen."

CHAPTER NINETEEN

What Does Normalcy Look Like

A couple days earlier, I noticed that Larry had a pink patch between his shoulder blades that itched terribly. It was a large blotch that was not raised at all, but just seemed to drive him crazy. He also developed some areas on the underside of his left arm that looked like broken blood vessels. Hydrocortisone cream helped, but he needed it about six times a day to keep the itching under control. The blotches would begin to look better and then they would worsen. One evening he said they had really started bothering him—not itching—painful. When he removed his shirt, the one blotch on his back was now two, and they were blistered. The underside of his left arm was blistered and so was the left side of his chest, right over his heart. I looked at this closely and thought to myself, *Okay, it's on his left chest, his left arm, and his left shoulder blade. It was itching and now it's painful and blistered. HMMMM.... Could it be??? Is it possible??? It was shingles. I was sure of it.*

I called the radiation oncologist on a Saturday evening and she immediately returned my call. She confirmed that what I was describing was indeed a severe case of shingles, which, unbeknownst to me, was common after what Larry had been through. Apparently,

THE GIFT OF TODAY

with all that radiation, a compromised immune system, and the stress of this disease, shingles were almost expected. I had no idea. She ordered an anti-viral medication that would reduce the spread of the virus by a couple days, but our pharmacy was not open again until Monday morning! *One of the down sides of living in a rural community is that stores are not always open when you need them.* In the meantime, I purchased over the counter remedies to make him more comfortable and dry out those blisters. I immediately called Les and Judy, because we had visited them in the past week, and Larry would have felt terrible if he had passed it on to one of them.

It seemed that every time we started thinking we were out of the woods and heading back to some type of normal life, we would find out differently. It just seemed to be one thing after another. Our faith was truly being tested.

I had taken care of patients in the hospital with shingles, but I had never seen a case get this bad before. Larry was absolutely covered in blisters and therefore, he went back on the strong narcotic painkillers. He said this pain was worse than the cancer pain. Those were not the words I wanted to hear. I was giving him oatmeal baths, which was an experience, because he was getting confused again and couldn't always understand when I wanted him to sit down in the tub. He would turn around and face backwards or kneel. He just wasn't always processing what I asked him to do, and he would get terribly upset about it. Sometimes kneeling in the tub just had to be good enough because he just couldn't understand "sitting." He said that bath felt so soothing. Then we would apply calamine, all to help dry up the blisters.

We started him on anti-viral medicine on Monday. Five enormous "horse pills" a day for seven days. I don't know how he swallowed those monsters. Being confined to the house, Larry became glued to the TV. He was bored to tears and needed something to do. I started talking to him more about this trip he wanted to take in March, and asked if he would like to incorporate a quick trip to Hollywood to see *The Price Is Right* in person. His eyes absolutely lit up. He loved that show! We sent for tickets over the internet and that really lifted his spirits. I would have loved for him to be chosen as a contestant. I wasn't sure he would be able to understand everything that was going on around him, but he sure would have had fun. It all depended on the day and the amount of stress he was experiencing. He could still understand anything mechanical and fix everything around the house, but couldn't understand a simple request like "sitting down in the bathtub." It was perplexing.

When we had taken our trip to Kauai in December, the airlines had sent us vouchers for additional airfare to be used in the future due to overpayment on our part. Airfares had dropped considerably after September 11th, and we had already paid for our Kauai trip, so they issued us vouchers that could be used up to a year later to fly elsewhere. With those, we could fly to California for the show, fly to Vegas and take in a couple shows, and then fly to Arizona to visit some of Larry's relatives. I knew this was a gamble in his confused state, but I had to try. I would have a week off work in late March, so we planned to go. It would be hectic, but I was willing to do whatever would make him happy. I believed that things would be better by then.

Friends stayed with Larry on Monday and Tuesday while I went to work. But, I was back home again on Wednesday because he had developed "the runs" during the wee hours of the morning from the anti-viral medication and we had a mess.

The day before, I had contacted the American Cancer Society for the first time. They advised me to take people up on their offers for help. That had always been a difficult thing for me to do. I didn't like asking for help because I thought it made me appear weak. Lesson: When we are at our weakest, God makes us strong and He brings people into our lives to see us through. I've heard it said that when you get to your wits end, that is where God resides. It was true.

THE GIFT OF TODAY

Ladies from my church were begging to help, so that day I put them to work. They went to the grocery store and post office, and then picked up prescriptions at the pharmacy. I also asked them to pick up adult diapers, which was a hard thing to ask. It was also hard to convince Larry to use those at that point, because he had lost all control.

Larry was resting comfortably by afternoon, but I kept encouraging him to drink fluids. That was no easy task. Sometimes he would get terribly angry and tell me to go away. I knew he didn't mean it. He was just plain sick of me nagging him about eating healthy, drinking fluids and not overdoing it.

That day he yelled at me, "Someday I'm gonna be the healthiest dead person around!" I tried to empathize with him, but to be honest, I couldn't begin to imagine what he was experiencing.

He barely ate, and was drinking Gatorade and water, but not in the quantities needed. For now, he had to continue taking the anti-viral pills because the benefits outweighed the risks. If we couldn't get that diarrhea under control, he would have to stop the pills. I hoped that would not be the case.

At this point, I was grateful for anything he ate or drank. We seemed to get his digestive system under control by late afternoon. He took his noon pill with only a small bowl of soup and a container of nutritional pudding, but seemed okay. By supper time, he was hungry and asking for food. I was thrilled. I ran through everything we had in the house and he settled on pancakes. I placed his evening pill next to his glass of water and prepared three large pancakes. He knew he had to have food in his stomach when he took that pill, and yet I turned my back for one moment, and he took the pill before eating the food. After eating two pancakes, he ran to the bathroom and threw up. He just didn't have any judgment anymore and it was my fault for not holding that pill back until he was done eating. I felt so bad that he was enjoying his food so much only to lose it all and become so sick.

Dianne Klancir

I called my supervisor and told her I could not leave him alone the following day and would not be in to work. I needed to find someone willing to keep him occupied a few days a week so I could work. There wasn't really much to do, other than making sure he was safe and that he took his pills with food, but I couldn't leave him alone. It's not that I felt I was so important at work that they couldn't do without me. We needed my wages. And, although my employer told me not to worry, I felt that I needed to be there whenever Larry didn't require my full-time attention. I anticipated taking months off down the road, and I needed that break away so that I could refresh myself to come back and deal with it all again. Caregiving was no easy task, but being the patient was much worse.

By Thursday night, I was physically and emotionally exhausted. We had an incredibly difficult day. Larry was vomiting and having diarrhea at the same time, and had not made it to the bathroom in time in either case on more than one occasion. His temper was getting shorter and I couldn't watch him go through any more of that. I called the radiation oncologist and explained what was going on. I told her I was not giving him one more of those pills. She agreed it would be best for his digestive system, but would not help his shingles to stop the medication. I explained that they had dried up fairly well, but the areas were so massive that they covered almost the entire left side of his chest and back, and the whole underside of his left arm. We continued with the calamine and oatmeal baths daily. It was an experience I would never forget. Some days I felt like I had been through a war by the time I got him settled into bed for the night. I would just lay there and cry and wonder how long I could continue to do this for him. I was afraid to close my eyes at night for fear he would awaken and in his confusion, fall down the stairs. I locked up his medication and hid it so that he couldn't get into that by mistake. It was overwhelming. With the viral pills discontinued, the diarrhea and vomiting also stopped.

THE GIFT OF TODAY

On Friday, a nurse's aide that I knew from the nursing home where Larry worked, stayed with him so that I could work. I was taken back with what she charged me for that duty, but it gave Larry a different face to look at and it gave me a break. The weekend went fairly smooth, although we didn't leave the house. Larry was rather testy and I thought it was better if he was angry with me and not others.

Tuesday was his appointment with the oncologist who had not seen him in a month. I was grateful to be off work for a holiday and able to take him to the appointment. But, it wasn't easy for one person to manage and I learned something valuable. Lesson: When dealing with a terminal illness, ask the doctor to write an order for a handicapped parking place if one is not offered. It will avoid the added stress of parking halfway across the lot and leaving your loved one at the door without you. Otherwise, you park the car, run inside for a wheelchair, wheel him inside and ask someone to watch him. Then, hope that he doesn't wander off or get angry while you're parking the car. Lesson learned!

The oncologist had no idea he'd developed shingles. She saw a very different Larry that day. I remember her expression when we walked into her office. She couldn't believe how thin he'd gotten and how confused he was. And, she couldn't believe the case of shingles he had. They were turning black and scabbing badly so she ordered special dressings to be done daily. I just kept wondering how much more his physical body could handle. We continued the pain meds as before and she told me to call if I needed anything else.

In the midst of all this, our computer of only two years had begun to act up. I noticed that there had been several pop-up screens that were coming up on our monitor and also some pornography that was absolutely disgusting. I couldn't figure out how that stuff was getting into our system. We had never looked up anything like that, but there it was sometimes staring us in the face when we went online. The system was running slower and slower, and it appeared we had obtained some kind of virus. The machine was also making a very scary sound that I had never heard before.

When Larry was first diagnosed, so many friends and family members wanted to know how he was doing, that I couldn't begin to keep up with all the letters and calls that would have required. So, I began journaling almost daily e-mails and sending them to a growing list of people. Over time it became an outlet for me; a very therapeutic outlet, as well as a way to keep people up-to-date. I could have never remembered the details of that time without these journals to refer back to. So, now my prayers were also for the continued operation of my computer!

"Dear God, this is my lifeline with the world. Please don't cut me off from my friends and family by taking down the computer. It is my source of communication with almost everyone. I will go crazy if I don't have e-mail to journal to my friends and family each day. Please, Lord, not my computer too!"

I alerted everyone that if they didn't hear from me for more than two days, it probably meant that the machine had died and I wouldn't have time to call people individually. Fortunately, the computer held on.

Thursday evening, Larry vomited before going to bed. That was rather surprising as he had stopped the meds that we thought were making him so sick. By Friday at 4:00 a.m., I was up with him as he was again having the runs. While I cleaned up, he fell back to sleep. I could not. I decided to call the oncologist to find out if he should be admitted to the hospital. He was getting so thin and I knew he had to

THE GIFT OF TODAY

be dehydrated. I was sure he needed IV fluids. It was just too painful to watch.

The oncologist asked to see him. Unfortunately, it was their first day in their new oncology clinic location. What a disaster! They were operational, yet they weren't. Half of what they needed was still at the old clinic and the other half was at the new one. It was quite stressful for all of us. Again I went through the hassle of obtaining a wheelchair, leaving him in the lobby, parking the car, and rushing back to him in the building. Larry had an extensive interview with the nurse practitioner, and then had lab values drawn. They gave him IV anti-nausea drugs and IV fluids with potassium. He rested well while they gave him fluids. I sat in a chair at his bedside and laid my head on the foot of the bed. Before I knew it, I was sound asleep too. No one bothered us. I guess they could tell we both needed the sleep. When he awakened, he was much perkier. I assisted him back into the car without an argument, and he even talked and laughed on the way home. I was so glad to see him coming around again. We had a long way to go, but he had made huge strides since that morning. His friend Earl dropped in that evening and they had a very nice visit talking about old times when we had been neighbors.

Dina came home for the weekend and insisted that she stay with her dad that Saturday and gave me some respite. She told me to go out and "have some fun." I couldn't imagine what to do, but Kris and I went to a movie, shopped and had dinner. It was great medicine for me. Bless my daughter's heart. In the midst of her pain, she found the time to relieve me of some of mine. I was so impressed with her thoughtfulness. I just wanted to hug her and not let go. I felt like she was dealing with so much of this alone and I felt so bad for her. She and her dad were still exchanging the journal that she had given him and it was their private communication. It was a great way for her to keep in touch with him and vice versa.

About 3:00 a.m. Monday morning, I woke up and felt like I had a rock in my stomach. As soon as I sat up in bed, I needed to make a run for the bathroom, and I began vomiting and couldn't stop. Larry woke up with another case of the runs and didn't make it to the bathroom. I now believed we had a bad case of the flu in the house, and wondered if we had stopped those anti-viral pills for Larry too soon. He spent the day on the family room sofa and I slept on the bed upstairs just to keep our distance from each other. We wanted so badly to banish this virus from our house because both of us could not be ill! I hadn't been to work in almost a week and now I was sick. Larry's shingles flared up badly that day too, and required more care. I was running on pure adrenalin. If it weren't for my journal e-mails, I would not have remembered many of these days. I was purely exhausted and had little recollection of the events of the day.

That night I moved into Dina's room so that Larry could have the entire bed and really stretch out. I thought it might help with those shingles. He balked at first that I wouldn't be there to hold onto, but I would hear him grimace in the night and thought that maybe he needed the bed to himself. I explained that I was right around the corner and that all he had to do was say my name, and I would come running. I couldn't even give the poor guy a backrub anymore because of the massive area those shingles covered.

About 2:00 a.m., I woke up and realized his bedroom light was on. I called out his name and there was no answer. I got up and ran into the bedroom to find him sitting on the edge of the bed with a huge pair of scissors I had never seen before, and a stack of his underwear. He was cutting them into shreds. I called his name but he didn't respond. I called louder, "LARRY!" He looked up with this totally spaced out expression and looked like he was going to cry. I asked, "Honey, what are you doing?"

"Well, I'm trying to help you. You work hard all day and I never do anything. I just wanted to help you."

THE GIFT OF TODAY

I started to cry. "Larry you have always helped me. You have taken care of me for 26 years. It has been a very full day. Why don't you finish this up in the morning and let me help you into bed?" I pleaded. He finally agreed and I tucked him back in. I took those scissors, wrapped them in duct tape and threw them in the outside garbage can, never to be seen again. To this day, I have no idea where they came from. Lesson: Search the house and remove all sharp objects from reach when someone is confused.

The following morning my "intestinal flu" flared up again. Larry was due at the oncologist's office at 7:15 a.m. He reported that his shingles felt good that day. (*Of course! It was his day to see the doctor. It's like when your car is running poorly or making strange sounds and you take it to the mechanic. Naturally, it runs like a top while you're there.*)

On the 40-mile trip to the oncologist's office, Larry became very confused and agitated in the car. I was so wiped out I could barely drive. He couldn't remember where we were going because he wasn't used to this new office location. When he saw the signs reading "Toll way 90 to Chicago" he removed his seat belt and dug through his pocket for a fistful of change. I asked what he was doing and he said it was change for the toll way. I explained that we were getting off before we got on the toll way and I didn't need the money. He became very annoyed and yelled, "Well, where the hell are you going anyway?" I tried to explain that we were going to the new office and he should just relax and rest. He pulled on the door handle and scared me half to death. I was afraid he would jump out of the car.

When we finally arrived at the clinic he couldn't figure out how to open the door anymore. He couldn't find the handle; he pounded on the window and yelled at me to open the door. I just stared at him in total disbelief. I had no idea that this could ever happen to my Larry. It was so unfair to him. It took forever to get him into the office and when we finally did, he made a grand announcement in the waiting room that his wife had almost killed him on the way over. It was heartbreaking.

The oncologist decided that the confusion was from the radiation to the brain and the steroid taper. The radiologist decided it was from taking the steroids and from the shingles. *Who was I to believe?*

The oncologist gave him two more medications. One was to increase his appetite (Megace®), per my request. The other was Lidocaine patches for his shingles. This would help reduce the pain. She also increased his dose of pain medication. He looked so frail, and the scale in the doctor's office showed he had lost another three pounds since his visit the previous Friday.

My situation had become somewhat better as I diagnosed myself with an ulcer and called my nurse practitioner to find out if she would concur. She did. It was no surprise to either of us that I had become ill. I was stressed to the point of breaking but wouldn't allow myself to admit it. She prescribed Prevacid® and I noticed almost immediate improvement. But, I had such abdominal pain that day when we got back home that I couldn't get out of the car right away. Larry went inside without me and was totally oblivious to my pain. I prayed that he wasn't getting into any trouble in the house.

He had gone to the mailbox and opened the mail. There were the tickets to the *Price Is Right* taping for March 28. He was so excited. I felt this deep gulp in my throat and wondered how in the world I would ever get him to Hollywood in this condition. If I did, what if he WAS picked to be on the show? It would be a disaster. I could only hope that with how bad his memory had gotten, he would forget about them. We had mentioned to the oncologist that we were scheduling another trip. She looked very surprised and said, "Make sure you get cancellation insurance this time." That said volumes to me. <u>Lesson: Take one day at a time and sometimes one hour at a time when you</u>

THE GIFT OF TODAY

are dealing with a terminal illness. Seize every moment that you can. Don't look back, don't look forward, just look up in faith and focus on the present. There is enough to deal with right there.

I continued to pray for the strength—physically, spiritually and emotionally—to wrestle with this crisis. While I always asked others to pray for Larry's health, now I also asked them to pray for mine. My tank was running on the big red "E."

It was now Wednesday, February 13th, 2002, and today our lives seemed to have turned around once again. I was so grateful for a good hour, a good moment, let alone a good day. The day was incredible and it just seemed that God's sense of humor was really evident. Dina arrived early in the morning and spent the day with her dad. She took the day off to be with him. As I have said before, it just made a difference in Larry's attitude when she was there. She was a fresh face, with a fresh attitude, a beautiful smile, and energy to burn. Just what he needed.

When I got home from work, he was smiling from ear to ear. They had a very special day together. She had made him breakfast and lunch, they watched *The Price Is Right*, and then she took him to the bowling alley where he usually bowled on Wednesday afternoons with his senior friends. He didn't bowl, but he got to see his buddies, laughed a lot, and got some fresh air. I was so proud of Dina for the way she looked after both of us through all of this. She had found an inner strength that just amazed me. So often when I was exhausted and out of energy, she arrived at just the right time. We were so lucky to have such a daughter.

My work had fallen quite far behind due to the number of days I'd missed. I just kept plugging away and knew that one day I would get caught up. It was really the least of my worries at that moment. My employer understood and never pressured me about anything. There was so much illness when I returned that day. Sixteen of our consumers were home ill and I had to send another one home. It was a bad year for colds and flu.

The following day our friend Bob, from church, was scheduled to be with Larry. He came from 8:30 a.m. until 1:00. That allowed me to work for a half-day. On Friday, some friends of ours asked to spend the day with Larry and take him to lunch in Rockford. I explained about his confusion, and they insisted they wanted to do this. We decided to see what Friday would bring. That was two days away and a lot could happen in two days.

The following day was Valentine's Day and as was our routine, we made arrangements to meet Dave and Eleanor for dessert together at a restaurant. After Dina's visit, Larry was totally up for the outing. She had no idea what a positive effect she had on her dad that day. His state of mind had changed to a more "pleasant state of confusion."

My sister Cathy and brother-in-law Mike from Wisconsin informed us they were coming to spend the weekend with us. We looked forward to that and hoped that Larry would feel like going out a bit. They had not seen Larry since Thanksgiving when we celebrated Christmas together as a family.

My sister Bobbie from Minnesota called to tell us she was coming to spend the following WEEK with us! What a Godsend! She and Larry had always gotten along so well, and Bobbie and I had always been close. I was so happy to hear she was coming.

It felt like a tremendous weight was being lifted off my shoulders. God kept sending people to ease this situation for us. I had very few episodes of pain and felt like my physical problems were improving.

However, Larry's son had a setback that day. He had problems weaning himself from the catheter after his surgery and now needed to have the catheter re-inserted. He was going to require more surgery to have scar tissue removed. He was very upset about that, but being his father's son, I knew he would have the right attitude to handle it when the time for the surgery came. In the meantime, we prayed that

THE GIFT OF TODAY

he would call upon the Lord to give him the faith he needed to rest on Jesus for comfort, patience and strength.

"I thank you Lord for a good day for my husband and for a daughter that has grown up to löve and respect her dad. I thank you for the opportunity to return to meaningful work and for an employer that understands what bears no understanding. Thank you for a beautiful day, a happier Larry, the gift of patience, a pain-free day for myself, and for incredible friends that never cease to amaze me. Thank you for ringing phones, for e-mail, and for doorbells that chime and tell us how lucky we are to have friends and family who care about us. In Jesus' name we pray. Amen."

CHAPTER TWENTY

Difficult Decisions

$\mathcal{V}$alentine's Day, 2002. It was one year from the day we had first noticed Larry's symptoms. I don't have to tell you that this Valentine's Day I had no expectations. I felt lucky that Larry agreed to go out for dessert that evening with our friends. I bought him a beautiful card and as I read it to him, he cried.

"I... can't believe...you still.... love me."

"I will always love you Larry. Just because we've had a few rough days, doesn't mean anything has changed. You will always be the love of my life," I said as I stroked his face.

We joined Dave and Eleanor for our Valentine's Day dessert ritual, but he barely participated in the conversation. I think it had become so hard to find words that he decided it was better to remain quiet. He was almost lethargic. At home, I helped him bathe and settle into bed. That was when the night turned into a disaster. He awoke during the night, incontinent of stool, rubbed it on the sheets and then because it was on his hands, left his mark on everything he touched in the bathroom. He used about three fourths of a roll of toilet paper and I awoke when I heard the toilet repeatedly flushing. The water level was just ready to go over the top of the bowl when I got there and began plunging for

THE GIFT OF TODAY

my life! The rest of the night was spent showering Larry and cleaning the bedroom and bathroom.

It was so painful to watch this happen to him. A person should be left with some shred of dignity, even when they are terminally ill. It seemed so unfair. I washed him again and settled him back into a clean bed and he immediately fell back to sleep.

This was all too incredible. Something had to give, and I was afraid it was going to be me. If I collapsed, who would take care of Larry??? As I cleaned, I thought back to different times in our lives. Finally, I just sat on the floor and cried, lost in my thoughts.

I remembered the guy who swept me off my feet and who made my heart flutter when he said my name. I remembered the man I fell in love with who was so strong and so eager to help others. I thought about the day we exchanged our vows and how I felt as if the sun rose on my life that day. I remembered the excitement on his face when he found out I was pregnant and how he wanted to be a part of Dina's birth. I recalled his laugh and ability to show his emotions and not be embarrassed about it. I thought about how he was always willing to do anything on the "honey do" list and plunged right in because his mission was to make me happy. I remembered some of our arguments and how foolish they seemed, how frivolous. I thought about how many times when Dina was growing up that he was the only man at the PTO meetings and it never bothered him. I remembered how excited and emotional he became at her first recital as she performed her tumbling and dance steps. I remembered how trusting he was in God when he retired with a minimal or no retirement fund and told me not to worry, that God would take care of us as He always had. What I remembered most was the man who was a good father to our daughter and a good husband to me – always faithful, always supportive, always loving. I remembered evenings he spent with Dina in the yard helping her pitch the softball. And I remembered that this man's one remaining dream was to walk his daughter down the aisle the day she was married. That terrific guy was still in there somewhere and I still loved him as much as I always had. He was a good man and he deserved so much better than what I was giving him. I saw a different physique and a different personality in front of me now, but this was the same Larry.

We had been blessed so many times yet rarely took the time to thank God for all He had done for us. We thought of God on Sundays, and whenever a tough situation came up, but we rarely said prayers of thanksgiving for all we had received. <u>Lesson: God shouldn't just be in our lives when we need Him. God deserves to be praised in our lives at all times.</u>

If we believe that God is there in the good times and we recognize Him then, why would we not believe He is present in the tough times? In our darkest moments, God is closer to us than ever, feeling every ounce of our pain, shedding tears with us. He deserves our worship, our love, our thanks. Whether we think of Him or not, He is always there to treat each day as a new beginning for us and forgive our sins if we will only ask. Why would we not be grateful for the gift of salvation that He has provided for us if we only believe? There is no greater gift.

I prayed over the right thing to do at that moment, finally deciding to call the oncologist and explain what our lives had become. I needed direction.

The following morning I called and asked her for total honesty about Larry's condition. "Can I expect to see improvement, or is this going to continue its downward spiral?" Basically, I needed to know if it was time for Hospice. If he was six months or less from death he deserved Hospice care. I wanted to be home with him at least the last few months of his life. The most important thing in the world was for me to be with him if he closed his eyes and passed away. I also

THE GIFT OF TODAY

wanted to know if he needed nursing home care or hospitalization, or if I would somehow be able to care for him at home.

Our house didn't have the greatest layout for someone who was confused—too many short flights of stairs and no bathroom on the main floor. We lived in a tri-level that we had designed and built. The living room and kitchen/dining area were on the first floor. There were two large bedrooms, two bathrooms and a utility room on the second floor, and a family room, bathroom and bedroom on the lower level. We also had an unfinished basement. So there were actually three flights of steps in the house. I was always concerned that he would wake up during the night and fall down those stairs.

I felt Larry was too weak to undergo any more treatments or tests. I had watched him lose eighteen pounds in the past forty days. The appetite stimulant (which was very expensive) worked one day and then stopped. He had a hard time holding his head up and even drooled at times. He was neglecting his left side since the shingles had appeared on that arm and didn't want to use his left hand. As a result, his hand swelled from time to time and we would prop it with a pillow and do therapy with that hand. His ankles were usually swollen by the end of the day and his color was looking ashen again. I needed to know if this was as good as it was going to get.

Her response was the one I dreaded..."It's time to call Hospice."

My heart sank. *How do you tell the person you love that his earthly life is almost over?* I was sure he knew it already, but it was one thing to suspect it and another to be told. It was too soon for all he had been through—just a year from the time he had been diagnosed. I gathered myself together and called Dina; another painful telephone call. She was going to Aurora that night to see Adam and decided to stop at our home on the way so that we could discuss this with her dad.

Less than thirty minutes after I hung up the phone with the oncologist, Hospice called. I postponed their visit until Dina and I had a chance to discuss it thoroughly with Larry and make certain he was comfortable with this decision. I also wanted to discuss it with Larry's son and daughter-in-law, Les and Judy. As I reached for the phone to call them, Judy called us. It was the day Les had his procedure to eradicate the scar tissue so that they could eliminate the catheter. The surgeon had difficulty removing the tissue and accidentally cut his bladder. He was now in the hospital on a morphine pump and the catheter was back in. The poor guy was really in pain. I felt awful bringing up this issue now, but I knew they would want to know the plans and how Larry's condition had changed. Judy understood and became tearful. It was not a good day for this family.

I was so relieved when Dina arrived. We discussed how to approach this, and then gently discussed it with Larry. We explained compassionately what the doctor had said, why she felt that way, and that we agreed with her. He sat there speechless and for the first time began to sob about his condition. A person with a brain tumor isn't always capable of rationalizing through situations, and he thought we were putting him into a nursing home because he was too much trouble. That sent me into tears. I felt so terrible and so guilty.

We explained that he was remaining at home with me and that no one was going to put him anywhere. (In fact, I explained that I was moving back into our bedroom so that he could hold me at night because I had gotten so lonesome in the other bedroom. That made him smile.)

We explained that Hospice was strictly to help with end of life issues and provide support for all of us. It was our wish to make him as comfortable as possible and share as much quality time with him as we could in the remaining months. We were not giving up on him. We were allowing him to have a voice in planning for the day when he would leave this earth and join his Heavenly Father. As Christians, we knew that this was the promise we had been given. At that point, he reiterated what he had said our whole married life—that when he passed away, we were not to restart his heart and he wished to be

THE GIFT OF TODAY

cremated. He also told me that he wanted his ashes spread at the fifth hole of the golf course. "That darned water hole gets me every time. I want to have the last word and be able to say, I MADE IT OVER THE WATER!" I assured him that I would honor those requests.

We explained that if he improved after Hospice began their services, we could always tell them they were no longer needed. However, if he felt that he could no longer hold on and was ready to close his eyes and meet his Maker, we would be there with him and so would Hospice.

I never wanted Larry to suffer and I never wanted his illness to be prolonged. In my heart I knew it was the right thing to do for him, for Dina and for me, but it was the most difficult thing I had ever done. Dina held up so well, holding her dad's hand the entire time. Sometimes I worried that she was being strong for me and wasn't allowing herself to express the sadness she felt. I was so grateful she had Adam in her life and he had been so good with her during those rough months.

I was really looking forward to family members being with us for the weekend and following week. I needed someone around to talk to once in awhile. Hospice was different from what I had imagined. I thought that they offered homemakers that would stay in the home and help with meals and stay part of the time with the family they were serving. That was not the case at all. They were incredibly compassionate nurses, but they required that the caregiver be there whenever they made a visit. So I continued to look for someone to stay with him occasionally during the day so I could go to work part-time, at least for another few days. The following week my family members would be there and that gave me great comfort.

Larry was still quite mobile, was not particularly short of breath, and aside from the intermittent confusion, was alert and communicative. I continued to pray for strength and God's will, as I knew this could go on for several months. It was without a doubt, a true test of my faith.

Friday night Larry's friend from work, Dick, stopped in to see him. Larry wasn't very talkative, but I know he appreciated Dick's presence. Visits were becoming very one-sided because Larry had so much difficulty saying what he wanted to say. Dina and I seemed to be the only ones he really felt comfortable conversing with. It was so kind of Dick to be a presence for Larry and watch a little TV with him. He offered to return the following morning so that I could run some errands, and he made breakfast for the two of them. That was so awesome! Dick will never know how much that meant to Larry or me. Larry ate everything on his plate.

Saturday afternoon, my sister Cathy and brother-in-law Michael arrived from Oshkosh, Wisconsin. It was good to see them. I knew that these visits were less than exciting for people so we appreciated them even more. We knew people were there because they WANTED to help. Even now, it's hard to express how much that meant, but anyone who has been in that situation understands. It was so important to know that people had not forgotten about us and that we were still very much in their thoughts.

Cathy insisted on making Larry a huge pot of chicken soup because she knew he loved homemade soup more than anything. I made my infamous apple crumb pie, which was his favorite fruit pie, and we feasted for supper. Michael brought his slide projector with them and we settled in to watch old family slides. We were having a ball and Larry laughed out loud at some of them. It was so good to see him having a good time. We had just gotten through a couple boxes of slides when the doorbell rang. There stood Bobbie, our kid sister from Minnesota. Then we really got serious about slide viewing! It was wonderful to have family around, to have something to smile and

THE GIFT OF TODAY

laugh about for a while to forget about cancer. <u>Lesson: There is joy in each day if we will only look for it.</u> Sometimes we have to search deeply and other times it hits us in the face. Take full advantage for you never know when it might be the last opportunity you have.

· The next morning we all slept in. It was the first time in weeks that Larry slept through the night. *I think he liked having me back in the bedroom.*

Later that afternoon, after Cathy and Michael had gone, our pastor delivered communion to Larry, Bobbie and me. It was a very peaceful visit and we always appreciated his gift of ministering to the sick. As I mentioned before, Pastor Mike was formerly a physician's assistant and had an innate ability to bring comfort to the homebound.

The following day I returned to work knowing that Larry was in excellent hands with Bobbie. He liked her so much. They used to tease each other so, and she wasn't about to let up on him now. She would give him such a hard time and try to get him going. He would just smile. He was being cooperative about eating his meals. He was in good spirits and was quite pleasant with my sister. I knew he appreciated her being there although he couldn't say it. Unfortunately, his confusion had not gotten better, but he HAD gotten better at storytelling. He was making up tremendous fabrications and filling in the blanks with whatever sounded best to him. One day he laid the TV remote control on the fireplace hearth and it melted. He accused Bobbie of ruining his remote control and had this long, drawn out version of what she had done. He kept asking her, "Why did you do this anyway?"

She had incredible patience. I was so grateful to her husband and three children for parting with her for a week.

.. That particular night was another challenge. It was his night for a shower. We changed off from showers to baths. By the time I was done helping him, I was wringing wet not only from the shower, but from the tears I cried trying to explain to him what we were doing. He did not understand and he was not cooperative. When my head hit the pillow, I was out like a light. About 2:00 a.m. he woke up and we had one of our typical middle-of-the-night conversations:

"Don't you hear the baby crying? Why don't you pick up the baby?"

"What baby?" I would ask half asleep.

"YOU DON"T REMEMBER THAT WE HAVE A BABY?"

"Oh alright." *I would pretend to get up and then come back to bed.* "Okay, I picked her up."

"IT'S A BOY!" he yelled.

"Oh whatever! He's fine now. Go back to sleep." *I couldn't believe I was having these conversations.*

"I'm hungry." *This, from the guy that I couldn't get to eat anything and had lost 18 pounds in the last 40 days.*

"Now?"

"Yea, I'm hungry."

"What do you want to eat?" *I played along.*

"What do we have?"

Oh God, please give me patience and the ability to fall back to sleep when this conversation is over. I remember running through the list of everything we had in the house and ending with hot dogs.

"HOT DOGS?" he yelled.

"SSHHHHH!! You'll wake the baby!" I responded.

"What baby???"

Then he would roll back over and go to sleep as if none of this had been spoken. That was the way our nights went. No wonder I was so tired at work I could barely function. Sometimes these conversations happened two and three times a night. Sometimes he would yell out or laugh or grimace for several minutes at a time. He would fall back to sleep and I would lay there awake wondering if he was alright. Unfortunately, I usually wasn't able to fall right back to sleep.

THE GIFT OF TODAY

The following day we called Hospice to get more details. Their intent was to do their intake assessment and have Larry sign the contract for their services. We prepared Larry that they were coming to talk and that he should listen to what they had to say. If he was uncomfortable with anything, we would not sign with them. He was friendly and receptive to the nurse that came, and seemed to understand what was said. We talked about going to Rockford the following week for four scheduled appointments, including the CAT scan. I questioned the benefit versus burden of those visits. I explained that it was getting harder to transport Larry to appointments. The nurse left that decision up to us, but it was understood that when Hospice's help was sought, no further treatments were scheduled.

Larry paused at that moment and said that he wanted to have the CAT scan to see if there was any improvement or anything else that could be done. The nurse and I tried to explain that he was in no condition for further treatment. He had gotten too weak. But because he hesitated, we didn't feel comfortable having him sign the contract for their services. We agreed to call the oncologist the following day and talk with her. I felt he needed to hear directly from her what the prognosis was before he would believe me. The Hospice nurse was very understanding and said she would return if and when we needed her.

The following day while I was at work, Bobbie drove Larry and the dog to the veterinarian. I couldn't believe she had gotten Larry into the car, but she said he was very concerned about the dog and wanted to be with her. Molly gouged the side of her neck the previous day while chasing a rabbit in the yard. Bobbie and I tried to clean it with peroxide but the poor dog jumped about three feet off the ground. So we left it in the capable hands of the vet.

Later that day, Bobbie planned to take Larry to the bowling alley to visit some of his friends. She began telling him who would be there. He couldn't place any of these people and decided he didn't want to go. She and I were both disappointed, but we didn't want to make him uncomfortable either.

Every day I encouraged Bobbie to walk him to the mail box at the end of our driveway, and then take him along the south side of the house to see if the crocuses were blooming. That gave him a little fresh air, a little exercise and a little sun. He was usually exhausted by the time he did that and it was probably a total of about 500 feet. The only thing he balked about was putting on layers of clothing to go out into the cold, because he caught a chill so easily.

On Wednesday afternoon, Larry's cousin Joe came for another visit. What an angel. He would sit and talk for what seemed like an entire afternoon and Larry barely had to say a word. He could make Larry laugh and that was worth so much to me.

Thursday, I attended a nursing seminar in Chicago all day. By the time I got home I was so tired. I walked in to a house that was spic and span. Bobbie had vacuumed, dusted, done the laundry and baked oatmeal raisin cookies for Larry.

I was trying to figure out what to make for dinner, and had thrown out several suggestions when Larry yelled, "MOOSE." I looked rather puzzled at why he would make such a strange request, and then figured out that he wanted to go to the Moose Club for dinner. I don't know if it was by coincidence, or if he somehow pieced together that it was "chicken night" at the Moose Club, but fried chicken was one of his favorite foods.

"Larry, we haven't eaten there in a long time because the chicken is fried and the atmosphere is so smoky. It's not good for you."

In a raised voice, he stated, "I'M DYING. CAN I PLEASE HAVE FRIED CHICKEN?"

He ate two whopping pieces of that chicken and an order of french fries. I knew in my heart this was not the meal to offer a cancer patient, but he was nearing the end of his life, and if this was what brought him happiness, then he was going to have it.

THE GIFT OF TODAY

On Friday, our friend Bob came at 9:00 a.m. and was still there when I got home at 3:00. He had visited with Larry the entire day and even stayed through Larry's naps in the recliner. Amazing. He did get Larry to play a couple games of air hockey, which absolutely wore him out.

That evening, our friends Dick and Diane, and Judy and Richard came with supper and stayed with Larry the entire evening so that Bobbie and I could have an evening out before she had to leave. Dina joined us. We had such an enjoyable time and the night slipped away so fast. We went to dinner, shopped and then returned to the same restaurant for dessert. We got home around 10:00 p.m. and I got Larry ready for bed.

Lesson: If you have a friend with a terminal disease, offer to spend time with them, or offer respite to the spouse. That is the most incredible gift of friendship a person can give. Provide a meal, send a card or flowers, but your presence is the best gift of all.

Our friends Alan and Kris came through for us again that week and ran an errand to Rockford to pick up a written prescription for Larry. They delivered it to the pharmacy and brought us a beautiful bouquet of flowers.

Saturday I took the car to the dealership for an oil change and because Larry insisted that the thermostat was stuck open. *Whatever that means.* The thermostat was not stuck open and because they couldn't find anything wrong, we had to pay the labor bill. *Ouch. Didn't need that.* I simply told Larry that they fixed it and thanked him for noticing.

Dina took a big step—moving from Madison to Aurora, a Chicago suburb, to share an apartment with Adam. She left her job and literally started over. We weren't happy about the living arrangement, but she was 24 years old and we certainly weren't going to tell her what to do. She was old enough to make her own decisions.

After a few incidents (lost keys and a flat tire on the moving truck) she and Adam were on their way. Adam was good about taking things in stride and they managed to laugh through the experience.

Saturday afternoon, Dina called and asked if her dad was able to come and see their apartment. Dina was always able to talk Larry into just about anything—including walking up three flights of stairs to see their new apartment. I couldn't believe it.

Bobbie, Larry and I drove to Aurora, all the while getting driving instructions from Larry. We just let it bounce off because he seemed to enjoy the scenery. We reminded him when we arrived that he hadn't walked up three flights of steps in a long time, and he should take it slow. In typical Larry fashion, he practically flew up the first two flights. Even though we made him rest at each landing, by the third, he was struggling. When we got to the top, his color was terrible, and he scared me. He snapped back quickly though, and would not admit that any of it was difficult. He was so excited to see Dina and Adam and he loved their apartment. They had all the conveniences—dishwasher, washer, dryer, fireplace, intercom system—the works. They really did look happy there and seemed to work together well. Larry ate better than he had in weeks, but that was because Dina cooked for him. No question.

Larry slept most of the way home and I showered him before going to bed. I applied lotion to his skin, which was so dry, and changed the dressings to his shingles. He had one spot that would not stop draining and stubbornly refused to heal. He slept like a baby that night. The ride and exercise proved to be good for him.

Bobbie was scheduled to fly home to Minnesota on Sunday. I nearly had a panic attack at the thought of her leaving. Instead, I took

THE GIFT OF TODAY

a deep breath, regrouped, and thanked her for being an angel of mercy. It was so sad to say goodbye. I felt blessed to have her for a sister.

Since Dina wasn't working now, she arrived Monday morning to spend the day with her dad. My parents were due to arrive sometime on Tuesday to help me out and I was so blessed to have all this help.

"Heavenly Father, I thank you for all the angels of mercy you have placed in our pathway and for showering us with your grace. I thank you for being a forgiving God who looks past our earthly behaviors and knows what is in our hearts. I thank you for Bobbie and I pray that she has a safe flight home and is returned safely to her family. I pray that you bless her family who sacrificed by allowing her to be with us in our time of need. I pray that Larry will realize we are in need of Hospice care for him and I pray that you will give me the hands, feet and heart of Jesus in order to lovingly and compassionately give care to my husband. In your Son's holy name I pray. Amen."

CHAPTER TWENTY-ONE

Just Call Us "Confusion" and "Exhaustion"

$\mathcal{W}$hatever relief I felt from Bobbie's visit quickly evaporated in the dark.

It was another bad night. Larry tossed and turned all night and between 3:00 and 4:30 a.m. talked loudly in his sleep. I didn't dare leave the bedroom and sleep in the other room, because I was afraid that he would wander around and get into trouble or hurt himself. Eventually, I cried myself to sleep thinking about my sister and missing her so much already. I was so relieved that Dina was coming the following morning early, and my parents would arrive two days later.

Dina arrived very early and I left for work. Larry woke up long enough to say goodbye to me and then fell back to sleep until 10:00 a.m. She tried to get him to eat but he only drank glasses of orange juice and water. When he wouldn't eat for Dina, we really had a problem. She brought out the old photo albums and tried to help him recall family events but he didn't even recognize himself in the pictures. He thought that I was a girl I used to work with and pointed

THE GIFT OF TODAY

at me, calling her name. When Dina told me what happened we shook our heads in disbelief at how quickly the confusion and memory loss were progressing. It was sad to see my life partner, the person I loved so much, deteriorate that way. *How could something this cruel and outrageous have happened to Larry? Damn that cancer!!*

Dina left that night and I could only pray that she'd get home safely and the forecasted snowstorm would bypass us entirely. My parents were enroute from Arkansas and hadn't driven through a Midwestern snowstorm in quite some time. I prayed for their safe travel, but also for their speedy arrival because I selfishly needed their support. Sometimes it got pretty lonely.

The next morning Larry had a range of appointments from a CAT scan, to blood work, to the radiologist, to the oncologist. I transported him everywhere by wheelchair because he was too weak to walk at all. He had recently developed hand tremors and was cold, pale and thin. It almost seemed hard-hearted to take him from place to place for all these appointments. But he insisted that he wanted to try this once more and I wanted to honor his requests. He was absolutely worn out by noon and so was I.

I guess you could say we had good and bad news that day. At least for me, it was startling news. The CAT scan showed that his brain tumors were gone. That's right—GONE! Normally, that would be reason for a huge celebration. It was definitely another miracle. However, I had to wonder, *why was he so confused?*

The radiologist felt his body had simply worn out from all the treatments. She said there was a slim possibility that he would improve slightly in a month, as the effects of the radiation wore off. I found that hard to swallow. She admitted that the high doses of narcotics he was taking, added to his confusion. I believed that. I also recalled when he was taking even higher doses and was confused to the point of cutting

213

up his underwear, yet still knew his name, address, phone number, and day of the week. He now needed re-orientation with everything but his name. There were no good answers.

From there, we went to the oncologist's office and had lab values drawn. They turned out much better than expected. (So far, none of this made sense). I asked if we could have a urinalysis to see if an infection was contributing to the confusion. I practically performed an acrobatic act to get that specimen from him. He didn't understand why the collection device was in the toilet, and wanted it out. Then we tried to collect it in the cup and he couldn't go. Next, we tried the urinal, and at first, that was a problem. When we finally succeeded I wanted to just throw myself down on the floor and laugh hysterically until I cried.

When the oncologist saw him walking down the hall toward the exam room she grabbed my arm. With a look of total disbelief, she uttered, "He looks like the walking dead," and her eyes welled up with tears. She and I sobbed together for the first time that day. She hugged me and said I had been a fantastic caregiver for Larry. I was very humbled by her statement. Larry told her how bad his pain had gotten from the shingles so she ordered a nerve block that would be administered at the hospital pain center. Unfortunately, they were too busy to see him that day, so.... another 80-mile round trip to Rockford had to be scheduled. But, we had a plan: If the nerve block was effective, wean off the narcotics and see if the confusion improved.

I tried to be hopeful that we would some day have the "old Larry" back again. However, because he continued to lose weight (50 pounds now since starting his treatments), his color was ashen, his balance, gait, level of consciousness and functional abilities had all deteriorated so much, the doctor believed the cancer had spread to other places. She and I both felt it would be barbaric to put him through any more treatments. Both doctors reiterated the need for Hospice care. It was what Larry needed to hear that day to know he was making the right

THE GIFT OF TODAY

decision. The oncologist offered to put him through further scans of the liver, adrenal glands and abdomen. At this point though, we had to ask ourselves exactly what we would gain other than knowing that the cancer was somewhere else. Larry was too weak to endure further treatments. The oncologist believed his belly was full of cancer. That was not the news I wanted to hear, and yet it wasn't surprising. Since we had no intention of seeking further treatment, I couldn't see subjecting Larry to another day like the one we just had. I didn't need to know where the cancer had taken up new residence. All I wanted to do was make my husband as comfortable as possible.

We refused the scans and the doctor understood completely. She said, "There are some people who have to know all the places the cancer has spread whether or not they pursue active treatment." We were not those people.

I was physically and emotionally drained by the time we got home. I couldn't begin to imagine how exhausted Larry was. Hospice was contacted and they agreed to be there at 5:30 p.m. Larry knew they were coming to make us official patients. We were not giving up, but rather learning to let go gently. We were still hanging on to hope. Once the nerve block was done and Larry was weaned off the narcotics, if there was improvement, we could tell Hospice we no longer needed their services.

"Lord God, I pray that Larry will be rid of his weakened state and confusion once he is no longer in pain from these shingles. As much as I selfishly want my husband here with me, I cannot watch him endure any more, and physically, he is unable to tolerate further procedures or chemicals. He has a wonderful life that awaits him with You. Lord, if this is all his poor tired body can take, I ask that in Your mercy, You do not prolong his pain and that You heal him in Heaven. One way or the other, I know You will heal, whether it be in this place or the next."

I was amazed that through all the weakness and confusion his sense of humor still made appearances. He would say some of the wildest things and let out an occasional "whoopee" when I said that if he drank his glass of water I would give him a Pepsi®. So we did still have our laughs throughout this time. He was the strongest man I had ever met. He didn't complain or ask "why me?" or want to be a burden to anyone. He was just plain tired. Yet he accepted each step with grace and dignity. It didn't seem right that with all the treatments and the disappearance of the tumors, that he should be left like this.

We were resolved with the decision to call Hospice. There was nothing we could have changed about this and I had to think about only those things we had some control over. I kept saying the Serenity Prayer to myself,

"God, grant me the serenity to accept the things I cannot change, the courage to change the things I can, and the wisdom to know the difference." (By Reinold Niebuhr).

Hospice completed their paper work with us and ordered oxygen for Larry with extension tubing so that I could take him from one level of the house to another without carrying the heavy oxygen concentrator up and down the stairs. It arrived the following day.

I was overjoyed to see my parents pull into the driveway that evening, but I'm afraid I was less than a great hostess. I was so tired by the time I got Larry to bed that I don't know what was keeping me upright. They couldn't believe their eyes when they saw Larry. My parents held back tears and did their level best to put smiles on their faces as they hugged him. They fully understood how tired we were and also retired early after a long day on the road.

It was another restless, talkative night for Larry. He thrashed in bed and actually hit me in the face once. Again, it was an almost sleepless night.

THE GIFT OF TODAY

The following morning the oncologist's office called to say they found blood and crystals in Larry's urine. There was no need for antibiotics, but they felt he was slightly dehydrated again, as I had suspected. The next day I brought him into the oncologist's office for additional IV fluids and then over to the Pain Center for his nerve block. He tolerated the procedure quite well. They inserted a long needle into his neck to deaden the pain at C-8 which runs across his chest and back, and down his left arm to his fourth and fifth fingers. But, he remained very confused and needed direction at every turn. He told the doctor he got some immediate relief. Then when we got home he wanted to elevate his arm on a pillow and asked for a pain pill.

That night after climbing the stairs to go to bed, he was so winded I put his oxygen on for the first time. During the night he pulled it off and awakened at 4:15 a.m. talking about writing $3.00 checks and asking if he had done the right thing. I reassured him and put the oxygen back on. He slept soundly until 9:00 a.m.

The following day we began having more computer problems and it looked like the machine was about to bite the dust. I kept praying that it would hang on and not let me down. It was getting crazier to use because we'd given the computer desk to Dina and now it sat on an old childhood play table and upside down crate. I didn't have the time (nor was it a big priority for me) to purchase a computer desk at that moment.

While my folks were there to watch Larry, I attempted to calculate our taxes and get that out of the way. It was just one of many things that needed to be done at that time.

Larry slept much better that night and I attributed it to the nerve block. *Praise the Lord!* He only had two pain pills the entire day and two Tylenol® before going to bed. He slept until 5:30 a.m. without waking up. That was exceptional! The next day he returned for a second nerve block and the doctor was very encouraged by the result of the first one. Larry started out the morning with Tylenol® again because he ate very little breakfast and said he didn't have much pain. He took a pain pill after lunch and another before bed and again made it through an entire day with no complaints. The Hospice nurse and I planned a weaning schedule for him with the doctor's approval.

That evening he talked with people on the telephone and made more intelligible conversation than he had in over three weeks. I was so encouraged. I was convinced the medications caused many of his problems—confusion, constipation, loss of appetite, somnolence, and vomiting.

The Hospice nurses were wonderful—patient, understanding and compassionate. By bringing the oxygen for him, they improved his breathing so much. He had really just gotten short of breath the week that Hospice was called.

On Sunday, the weather was bitterly cold and icy so we decided not to attend church. Our pastor called to ask if he could deliver communion to us. We were so blessed and continued to hope that Larry would overcome this. I didn't know many people who could have tolerated what Larry had. I constantly reminded our friends to tell their life partner how much they loved and needed them in their lives, to make each moment count and celebrate that..."this was the day the Lord had made, to rejoice and be glad in it." Psalm 118:24.

CHAPTER TWENTY-TWO

Bittersweet March, 2002

On March 3rd, our neighbors came over in the bitterly cold weather with shovels and a snow thrower, to clear our entire driveway and sidewalk. We were totally oblivious to their efforts. I bundled up to brave the cold, and was greeted with that wonderful surprise as I prepared to hand shovel the entire driveway.

That afternoon, our friend Bob called to ask how many people were at our house. When I told him there were four of us, he said, "Well, lunch is on the way so don't make anything. I'll be right there." Moments later, he arrived at our house with piping hot huge baked potatoes brimming with broccoli and cheese sauce and fresh vegetables on the side. Mom and I appreciated that because we were busy preparing a big supper for later on when Dina arrived. Larry was having a pretty decent day with few complaints of pain and was less confused. He slept a considerable amount, but as long as he was comfortable, I didn't care.

Dina arrived with Adam about 4:00 and by 5 p.m., my mother had put a spread on the table that resembled Thanksgiving. We had turkey, stuffing, gravy, sweet potatoes, green bean casserole, tossed salad and cranberry sauce. She made a pineapple upside down cake and chocolate éclair for dessert. We hadn't feasted like that in a long time. It was all so good and even Larry, who wasn't eating enough to satisfy a bird, smothered everything in gravy and ate a heaping plate of food. Dina and Adam left about 9:30 p.m. but Dina thought she might be back on Tuesday to help me take her dad to his next nerve block appointment.

Larry's cousin Joe, whose company we enjoyed so much, spent the better part of Monday afternoon with Larry before he and his wife Marilyn left for an extended vacation. I knew Joe had a million and one things to do -- getting the motor home packed and closing up the house -- but he thought of Larry first. That was so special to us both. It was so generous of his wife, Marilyn, to share him with us when there were so many other tasks that needed his attention.

Larry was visited by six coworkers that day. They brought an entire lunch to our house and Larry's friend Dick who is very comfortable in a kitchen, came early to prepare things before the other guys arrived. It sounded like they had a wonderful time. They had him belly laughing, reminiscing about days working together in the Maintenance Department, and he ate well again. That gesture was so good for Larry's spirit. We thought the world of those guys. May the Lord bless them for their unselfish acts of kindness toward my husband.

The Hospice nurse visited and brought a bubbler for Larry's oxygen that would add humidity and keep his nose from getting too dry. She changed the dressings to his shingles, and the area that had been draining was now healing. Things were really looking up.

Dina would arrive the next morning to help me take her dad to his third (and hopefully last) nerve block appointment. My parents were running errands and keeping up our household for me. I wanted to give them a day to themselves as they had been cooped up in the house for a week without a break. That night as I e-mailed our friends, I wrote

THE GIFT OF TODAY

the following: *"May you all be blessed with angels in your lives that help you realize you are never alone in these situations. The Holy Spirit provides us with comfort in so many ways. Sometimes it is hard to see the bigger picture, but I know there is good in this. We have come to know what deep friendships we have, what caring people we both work with, and what the warmth of God's tender love feels like. I know He is with us through every step of this, helping us realize that as things get tougher, we need to rest on His shoulders more. There is no way a human being can survive this type of situation and not feel God's presence in all of it. We know God heard our prayers and the prayers of friends and family all over this country and Mexico for Larry. He is on more prayer chains that I could even begin to tell about. Those prayers have given him the strength to endure what he has this past year, and have removed those tumors from his body as they were treated. Those prayers gave us valuable time together that we never thought we would have had a year ago. We are indeed fortunate and grateful. We are wrapped in the warmth and grace of God. Blessings to all you angels; you are special beyond measure. God's love and mine, Dianne."*

It was so therapeutic for me to write to everyone almost every day and express in words what was happening.

The next day Dina and I took Larry to Rockford for the third nerve block injection. Dina got to see first-hand how "interesting" it had become to transport Larry anywhere. It was definitely a challenge. The doctor was very patient with Larry and diligently tried to get a handle on exactly where Larry's pain was so that he could provide the most relief. Larry was not very helpful describing the pain and its location. He would change what he told the doctor from one second to the next. Not intentionally, he just couldn't describe what he was feeling. It was so difficult for the doctor and me to know if he was really being helped by this or not. He would say he felt much better and had no pain and then turn to me and ask for a pain pill. We finally decided that when he began saying that the underside of his arm was hurting that would be an indication of how long the nerve block was effective.

Dina pushed Larry's wheelchair back out to the car, taking the scenic route through the hospital so that he got to see something different. Once in awhile, she would bend over and give him a peck on the cheek. He would just grin. She was a champ through all of this, and a great support to me. Dina dropped me at work for a couple hours and then drove Larry back home where he slept away the afternoon. When I got home, Dina was visiting with my mom and dad, who got to spend a relaxing day together going out to lunch, shopping, and visiting some old friends in the area. Larry was passed out on the couch and Dina was back on the road to Aurora by 5:00 p.m.

Larry slept well that night, but by Wednesday complained of arm pain and asked for a pain pill. I called the doctor who said that there was no point coming back for any more if that was how long the nerve blocks lasted. His fear, from the beginning, was that we had waited too long. He wished we had been offered those injections earlier.

Our hope of getting Larry off narcotics was shattered. He began requesting painkillers more and more frequently. He now used oxygen about 50 percent of the time and I was amazed at how short of breath he had become in the last couple weeks.

The following two days I had to attend mandatory workshops in Elgin for abuse and neglect reporting to the Office of Inspector General. I would have rather been anywhere but there. Typical state crap—red tape and abuse of time. What took two days to accomplish could have been done in four to five hours. When I arrived home, our friend Dale was there with gifts from his wife Carol's kitchen. My folks had taken care of Larry the past two days and they made Dale feel right at home. Carol sent a huge plate of individually wrapped pizza burgers, a tub of BBQ, a casserole and homemade cookies. It was all delicious. My friend Shirley sent a casserole right out of her oven

THE GIFT OF TODAY

that evening so after returning from an exhausting day of listening to lectures and then a long drive home, it was such a treat to sit down to a prepared meal. My mom appreciated it too as she had been care giving all week.

Later, one of our daughter's girlfriends, Erin, stopped in for a visit. I was so impressed that she took the time to do that. She had always been a breath of fresh air and her presence would light up a room. Larry truly appreciated her thoughtfulness.

That evening, Larry complained more of pain and seemed more short of breath. Friday morning, I called the Hospice nurse and asked her to call the oncologist. I wanted to give him a ProCrit® shot to boost his red blood cell count, which would take about ten days to really take effect. It seemed that he didn't have enough circulating red blood cells because the oxygen wasn't always relieving his shortness of breath. The oncologist agreed that I could administer the shots because I had ProCrit® in the house. I was to give him one per week until it was gone and monitor his breathing.

About 4:00 that afternoon, three guys from the Forreston Lions Club came to the house to present Larry with the 2002 Emeritus Award from their club, for his years of service and dedication to their organization. Larry was speechless. They also gave him a $100 check for the Pinecrest Good Samaritan Fund for which Larry had always canvassed donations. The following evening was the bowling benefit for this fund and I was going to surprise Larry and bring him over there to present the check himself. The guys stayed for a visit and brought donuts and coffee to share with Larry. They took pictures and one appeared in the local newspaper. I was very touched by their compassion and recognition of my husband's efforts. Larry, of course, was very humbled by the entire visit.

That night my parents packed their van to return to Mountain Home, Arkansas. The following morning they left bright and early. It was so helpful having them at the house and we all became quite emotional when they departed. I know it was as difficult for them to leave as it was for me to say goodbye. Their stay allowed me to work part of the time and not have to worry about what was needed at home. Mom did most of the cooking and cleaning. Dad vacuumed one day for me and cleaned my exhaust fans in the bathrooms. They were so comforting to Larry and kept him involved in card games, dice games, conversation, and reading his mail, so that he wouldn't sleep all day and then be awake at night. I was so grateful they could be with us for a while. I prayed for their safety on the road and their safe return home. It was mind-boggling to think of how we were going to handle our lives with all these people gone now. Between family and friends, we had received so much assistance, and it made our lives so much less complicated. It gave us more time to spend together when I got home; talking, listening to restful music, and enjoying the comfort of each other and our lovely home.

Amanda Bradley has such an eloquent way of saying things. She writes, *"God bless the friend who sees my needs and reaches out a hand; who lifts me up, who prays for me and helps me understand."* That is truly a friend. We had been showered with many.

Some of our closest and dearest friends were either on vacation at this time or were going on vacation the following week. I knew Dina and I would not have much help to get through the next week.

On Sunday, March 10th, my parents called to say they had arrived home safely. My friend Shirley sat with Larry a couple hours that day so that I could get some things at the store and pharmacy. When I got home, I completed the taxes and finished up laundry. Larry got very short of breath that evening, so I laid with him on the couch and held him. I stroked his back gently and we listened to relaxing music by the fire. He was working harder to breathe. I decided to call our church friend, John, who had offered to spend the following day with

THE GIFT OF TODAY

Larry, and tell him I was staying home. I didn't feel that I should leave when he was so short of breath, which also caused him to be more confused.

On Monday, March 11th, Larry slept later than usual. When he got up, I showered him and awaited our visit from Hospice. They came for their usual morning appointment and realized they were out of dressings for his shingles and needed to make a second visit that day. While they were there, I got to sit and really discuss some important issues with the nurse. I told her I was concerned about the shortness of breath and wondered if it was time for me to take a leave of absence and stay home with Larry. I told her I wanted to be home with him the last couple months and wondered if she had any idea, based on her experience, how close we were to that point. She was very non-committal, but didn't seem as concerned as I was. Larry was a fooler. He would have a couple days when he appeared to be down and out, and then he would bounce right back. He was going to live right up until the moment he died, and praise God for that!! It did, however, make it hard for anyone to predict when I should finally stay home with him and how long he could go on that way.

I remember that day that Larry slept a great deal on the couch in front of the fire and TV. I could barely get any food into him at breakfast or lunch. I had been given a nursing journal a couple years earlier for my birthday, and whatever made me pick it up that day, was beyond me. I had never really looked at it before. I made one entry in this journal as follows:

"3/11/02 - I dedicate these pages to my husband Larry and my daughter Dina. It is a beautiful sunny, crisp Spring day and to look outdoors, it would seem that all is right with the world. I am home from work because my husband needed me more than my job today. My husband has battled lung cancer that metastasized to the soft tissue of his spine and then to his brain. He was diagnosed origi-

nally on February 17, 2001. He has endured painful procedures, months of chemo and radiation and has now become too weary to tolerate anymore. His body and mind are tired and it was time to say, ENOUGH. My only wish for Larry each day is that he is comfortable. We are having some difficulty achieving that end some days, but we are plugging away trying. The Hospice nurses who were ordered by Larry's oncologist on 2/26/02, have been very supportive. I am grateful to have them in our lives. They have visited here twice today. Both times it was Sue that came, and on her first visit she had a medical student with her. Larry's color was dusky/ashen looking today. I tried to give him every opportunity to rest that I could, and he slept on the sofa with his oxygen on almost all day. He barely ate or drank anything. I would occasionally rub his back and we had minimal conversation, but I do remember hugging him and crying and telling him how sorry I was that this happened to him. His response was "I'm sorry I'm putting you through this."

At that point, for some reason, I chose to stop writing. I sat on the couch and rested his head in my lap. I stroked his hair and sang to him softly. At 5:30 p.m., the telephone rang and it was our daughter, Dina.

"I have some incredible news!" she exclaimed. "Put dad on the phone too, mom."

It took awhile to get Larry seated, hand him the phone, then go into another room to pick up a different phone, but we finally got ourselves situated.

"Okay, what's up?" I asked intently.

"Are you both there?" We could hear the excitement in her voice. Larry responded, "Yes, punkie, I'm here. What's going on?"

"I'M ENGAGED TO ADAM!!!" She screamed. "We went out today and picked out the ring, and it's incredible. I can't wait for you to see it but it's being sized. I'm so happy." She was absolutely floating.

Larry and I yelled, "Oh gosh! Congratulations!" We were pleased

THE GIFT OF TODAY

at the thought of having Adam as our son-in-law. We really hadn't had time to think much about that relationship and how serious it had become. Dina couldn't wait to see her dad and me in person. Larry worked hard to speak but he told her how happy he was for her. Adam was working that evening so we didn't get to speak to him. It was so much fun to receive some good news in our family.

"Thanks for the wonderful news. We love you. Tell Adam we love him too," I said.

"Love 'ya ….punkie," Larry weakly uttered.

"Love you guys too. I'm so happy," were her last words before hanging up.

When I came back downstairs, Larry was already laying down with the phone in his hand.

"Well, what do you think of that?" I asked him.

"I knew…. he was…. nuts…. about her." He struggled to say.

"Adam will be a good son-in-law," I responded with tears of joy running down my face. He seemed to really want to please our daughter. She had stars in her eyes for him from sixth grade on. They seemed like a perfect match.

I went to the kitchen to heat a bowl of soup. Although I wanted to bring him a dinner tray, Larry insisted upon going up the stairs to the kitchen to eat. It took so much effort just to help him stand. As we started to walk, he became very unsteady, and I felt him falling from my arm. I tried to catch him the best I could, and I was able to keep him from falling all the way to the floor, but he just dropped like a rock. I looked at his face and saw his eyes roll back. He tried to say something, but his words were garbled. It was then that I realized the seriousness of the situation. I tried to find a pulse, but there was none. I yelled out, "Larry, don't leave me. Please, don't leave me!"

I lowered his head to the floor, checked for a pulse again, and when there was none, I ran for the telephone. I wildly punched numbers into the handset, calling our pastor and the Hospice nurse. I asked them both to come quickly and just said, "Larry is taking his last breaths," in a totally frantic voice. I raced back to him and checked again for a pulse.

There was none. I felt for respirations against my cheek. There were none. He was gone just that quick. No warning. No good-byes. No last "I love you's." He was gone.

I laid there next to him sobbing out loud waiting for my help to arrive. I sat on the floor and rocked him in my arms and told him "I love you" at least a hundred times. I never wanted to let go. I couldn't believe that a half hour ago we were talking to our daughter on the telephone and sharing her wonderful news. After all we had been through, it was over before we had a chance to really say good-bye. I was so grateful that I had been home with him and we had that precious day together. The man I loved with all my heart for 27 years was going on to another life without me. At that very moment, all I could think about was that I wanted to go with him. I didn't want to be here without him.

Our doorbell rang and it was our pastor. He raced downstairs and touched Larry and could see he was no longer alive. He gave a blessing to him and his eyes welled with tears. He knew all we had been through. We just stayed there and held Larry together. After what seemed like an eternity and was actually about another ten minutes, the Hospice nurse arrived. He checked Larry's respirations and pulse. "He's gone," he stated sadly. He called the oncologist who pronounced him deceased at 6:32 p.m. There was no need for a coroner's case when Hospice was involved.

The Hospice nurse called the funeral director to come to the house. I was still holding Larry and crying. I kept stroking his hands and face. Pastor asked whom he should call to come and comfort me. I asked for my friend Kris, but asked him to call Dina first. She would need someone with her. I prayed that Adam would be able to drive her here because I didn't want her driving.

THE GIFT OF TODAY

I remember saying over and over again to Larry, "I loved these hands," as I stroked them. Those hands brought so much comfort into my life. Now, they would no longer be there for me. I would continue to be in the comfort of God's almighty hands, and although that should have felt so restful, at that moment, I only wanted my Larry back again. I would only have fond memories of Larry now.

I was sobbing so hard I could barely catch my breath. The Hospice nurse became concerned and took my blood pressure, which was quite elevated.

"Dear Heavenly Father, I know there is a reason for all this, and I know Larry is already with You. Part of me is so happy and so envious that he is in such a beautiful place with his eternal Father. I long to be there with both of you. My heart is breaking and I don't know if I can go on without Larry. Give me the words to tell my daughter that this has happened. This should be the happiest day of her life. It will be the most bittersweet instead. Lord, help me to understand how precious life is and how quickly it can be taken. Help me to endure the pain I am feeling right now. I ask You to be with Dina and me and give us guidance and healing. Thank you Lord for not allowing Larry to suffer any more. It was a quick, smooth transition into the next Life, and I would have wanted it that way for him. Yet, the selfishness inside of me wants him back. He was a good man and I was so blessed to have him in my life. I thank you for bringing him to me, and for now giving Dina and me our own private angel. Lord, I ask for strength for Dina and me. We are hurting right now even though we know that Larry is no longer in pain and is already healed. We ask you to give us the strength that only You can provide. In your Son Jesus' holy name. Amen."

When I looked up, the house was filled with people. At least 30 people had already gotten word of Larry's passing and had come to offer their condolences. Larry's friend Dick had made coffee for everyone and people just kept coming in the door. The pastor and

Hospice nurse had convinced me to release Larry and laid him on the sofa. I watched him lay so peacefully. I was certain he would open his eyes and be back with me.

Friends continued to come. Kris arrived and we cried together. She wrapped her arms around me and it felt so good. She and my friends were busy calling people and passing the word. Before I knew it, Dina and Adam were there. Dina was upset when she walked in and saw all those people in our house.

"What are all these people doing here?" she asked. We hugged each other and cried and Adam hugged me with tears in his eyes. "I'm so sorry, mom" he said. *I loved to hear him call me mom.* I explained to Dina that these were all our close friends and they wanted to be there to comfort us and let us know we had their support and love. She was not expecting anyone to be there except us and it took her by surprise. She went into the room where Larry lay and gave him her final kiss. I followed her in and did the same.

She and I were escorted upstairs by the funeral director, who had some very specific questions for us about what our wishes were for a funeral. Larry and I had spoken many times over the years about our desire never to be resuscitated if our hearts stopped, and to be cremated after death with just a memorial service. I was so relieved that in the midst of what was happening that I remembered those details. So much of that evening was a blur.

There was a sad irony that Larry passed into Life on 3/11. Three was always Larry's lucky number, and eleven was mine. What an incredibly lucky day to be taken to his eternal home. Lucky for Larry.

That evening Dina sent the following e-mail to friends and family who had not already been notified of her dad's passing: *"Hello everyone. This is Dina. Unfortunately, I am writing to tell you that my dad passed away this evening. It was very sudden but we thankfully*

THE GIFT OF TODAY

had the support of our friends and family here. Mom is understandably upset, but holding up okay. There will be no funeral or visitation. Dad requested cremation, and there will be a memorial service for him sometime this week or weekend. Mom will e-mail you with more information about that. Thank you all for your thoughts and prayers through this difficult time. It meant so much to us. Sincerely, Dina."

It was late when our friends left for the evening. I was so relieved that Dina and Adam were there with me. We were all exhausted, yet I didn't want to close my eyes to sleep, and I didn't want to go to bed alone. I decided I would stay on the couch downstairs and see if I could fall asleep. Dina wanted to stay with me but I assured her I would be okay, and she and Adam went upstairs to sleep. I remember turning on the TV just to have some noise; the silence was deafening. I kept looking around that room and remembering what had just happened. Part of me was hurting so badly I didn't think I would make it through the night. Part of me was so relieved that he was no longer in pain that I felt like a lead weight had been lifted. It was difficult to explain.

About halfway through the night I finally fell asleep. When I awoke I wandered upstairs to the living room and sat on the sofa. The living room windows faced east. The most beautiful sunrise became visible to me. It was so bright it was almost blinding me through the window. I sat there with tears in my eyes, and knew that God was reassuring me that everything was beautiful, Larry was safe, and my life would go on with His help.

CHAPTER TWENTY-THREE

The Final Chapter

*I*sn't it amazing how life can change so quickly? Isn't it astounding that we had over a year to prepare for this and when the end came, it was still a surprise?

I was so grateful for those thirteen months in which God had worked in me and helped me to let go gently. But a piece of me died the day Larry died. My heart felt like it had been broken beyond repair. I don't think I truly realized what an extraordinary life we had until he was gone.

The next couple days were a blur. I remember that Dina and I went to the funeral home Tuesday morning to help write Larry's obituary. There were so many details they wanted to know and I couldn't remember anything. Fortunately, the funeral director was very patient and kind. He understood those moments that people experience in their mourning. I would stare off into space, and he would gently bring me back to reality by calling my name and touching my hand. Larry and I had never talked about his obituary. To be perfectly honest, I never thought about it. I don't know if it was positive thinking, or if we were just so busy enjoying our lives while we were able to, that it wasn't something we wanted to think about. Toward the end, we were busy

THE GIFT OF TODAY

attending to Larry's needs and his confusion level didn't warrant that type of discussion. At times Dina and I had to pull ourselves together to complete the information, but we finally did it.

We had spoken to our pastor earlier that morning and confirmed that Saturday would work for Larry's memorial service. Arrangements for cremation were made with the funeral director and Dina sent an e-mail informing everyone of the memorial service, Saturday, March 16th at 11:00 a.m. We had established four memorials in lieu of flowers: one to our church, one to my employer, one to Larry's employer, and one to Hospice. We didn't want to leave anyone out.

That afternoon we met again with Pastor Mike, who helped us through the arrangements for the memorial service. We chose Bible verses, music, a vocalist and an accompanist. Pastor talked to us about the eulogy. He had learned so much about Larry during his illness and I was very touched by his warm impression of my husband.

Sometime early that week, family arrived—Cathy, Margie, Bobbie, my parents, and Les and Judy. Food appeared almost hourly and cards began arriving in massive quantities. Bobbie and I took some of our favorite photos of Larry to a local store that enlarged pictures and added borders. We had Larry's military photo enlarged to an 8" x 10" with a red, white and blue border. We enlarged a photo of Larry in a tuxedo from several years ago, and then picked one of him in the last months of his life sitting in his golf cart. They were all placed in beautiful silver frames for his memorial service.

Wednesday evening we all gathered at my home for dinner. My friend Kris had provided the entire meal for all of us–salad, garlic bread, lasagna and dessert. She even brought extra paper products like napkins, kleenex and toilet paper because she knew how many people were staying at my home. That was so thoughtful.

My sister and I bought champagne that day, so that in the midst of this loss we could toast Dina and Adam's engagement. It was a difficult thing to do, but I felt their joy should be celebrated. So, at dinner that evening I asked everyone to raise their glasses, and we toasted Dina and Adam's good news. Somehow I managed to get the congratulatory words out without falling apart and crying. I knew Larry was there in spirit and would have wanted us to do exactly that. Dina and Adam were amazed that we thought to do that for them. I was so glad we did.

My sister Margie brought a spiral notebook for me that proved to be invaluable. Every time I spoke to someone on the telephone, we logged it in that book. Every time someone brought food to the house she asked them to sign the book and note what they brought. Each time someone called, she logged it. I also recorded everyone who sent memorial gifts. Later, when the fog lifted, I went back to that book repeatedly to write thank-you cards. I would have never remembered the information without that notebook. It was a wonderful idea and I was so grateful to her for bringing it.

Lesson: Do not count on your memory at a time like that. Have someone close to you take responsibility for helping with those details. Make a log of all phone calls, gifts of food or money, visits, flowers, and use it religiously so that you can refer to it later and thank people appropriately.

Margie also intercepted many calls for me and took messages, as there were times I wasn't emotionally able to speak. Sometimes I needed to take a nap in the middle of the day, and she didn't want to wake me because I had not slept well the night before. I really appreciated her take-charge response to that situation.

One evening, the family spread out pictures of our 26 plus years together on the living room floor. Les brought pictures of his dad from long before I knew him. We all spent the evening putting together posters of Larry's life, with captions to accompany the pictures. It was a great team effort and allowed us shared moments of laughter and tears. In the end, they captured Larry beautifully.

As was the custom, the women's group at our church offered to serve a luncheon following the memorial service. They told us not

THE GIFT OF TODAY

to worry about a thing except to give them some idea of how many people to prepare for. *How does a person know something like that?* We knew that several of our closest friends were on vacation. We knew that most people had Saturdays off, but we had no idea if they planned on attending. So, we picked a number that sounded good–220 people. As it turned out, we weren't far off. *And, as I always said, it was better to have too much food than not enough.*

It was difficult for some people to attend such services and we fully understood that. I had been in those shoes before, and knew it was not easy. Now I make a point of attending as many funerals of friends or family as I possibly can, because I know how much it meant to Dina and me that people took time out of their busy weekend to attend Larry's service and luncheon. It provided so much support for us at such a difficult time in our lives.

It was Saturday, March 16, the day of the memorial service, and I thought I was so prepared. As we arrived at the church and I began to see some of the people who had come to share in our grief, I became quite emotional. My entire family was there, including my mom and dad, three sisters and their families, and Dina and Adam. Larry's eldest son and his family were in attendance, as well as his other son and daughter and her family, whom we had not seen in years. Larry's only brother and sister-in-law, and niece and nephew and their families were present. I was overjoyed that they chose to pay their final respects to Larry, but he would have appreciated spending more time with them when he was alive. Those opportunities are forever past now. <u>Lesson: Moments need to be seized; every day needs to be treasured and used to the Glory of God; and life is too short to be in the presence of negative energy or people who always see things on the dark side.</u> I believe this is something I finally "got" when I experienced the death of an immediate family member.

Larry's service was beautiful. Pastor gave the invocation and everyone sang "You Have Come Down To The Lakeshore," one of our long-time favorite songs. Some of the words are, *"You have come down to the lakeshore, seeking neither the wise nor the wealthy, but only asking for me to follow. Sweet Lord, You have looked into my eyes, kindly smiling You've called out my name. On the sand, I have abandoned my small boat, now with You, I will seek other seas."* ©

The song sent me into tears and I was sobbing loudly. Larry would not have wanted me to cry at his service. I'm afraid I disappointed him. He would have wanted it to be a celebration of his life and that was the way the pastor preached about him. The scripture reading was 2 Timothy 4:6-8, *"For I am already being poured out like a drink offering and the time has come for my departure. I have fought the good fight, I have finished the race, I have kept the faith. Now there is in store for me the crown of righteousness, which the Lord, the righteous Judge, will award to me on that day--and not only to me, but also to all who have longed for his appearing."*

Pastor spoke of Larry as a man of integrity, a man of his word, a faithful husband and father. He spoke of Larry's generosity in helping others, his gift of craftsmanship, and his faith throughout his illness. In the end, he noted that Larry often wore a smile, even on some of his worst days, and that he had indeed fought the good fight. He then read a letter to the attendants that I had written to Larry one sleepless evening that week as I lay and watched the sun come up through my living room window. He fought back tears as he read,

"My dearest Larry,

I wasn't planning on falling in love when I met you, but it seems God had other plans. Many people said our relationship would never last because of our age difference. In the music of life, I thought we made beautiful harmony. You were a great listener, I was the talker. I was the planner, and you knew how to carry out those plans. When I sought higher education you were the support system cheering me on. You were my lover, my best friend, my companion. Your strong hands always gave me a sense of security and comfort. Now when I am alone, I will feel your presence in a different way. You will still

THE GIFT OF TODAY

always have a place at my side, and now the security I feel will be the presence of my own private angel.

I am so proud of our accomplishments together, but mostly for the daughter we raised. I know you are especially happy about the future she is entering into with Adam.

We have been through so much together and with each obstacle, we seemed to emerge stronger. You have shown me what a quiet, unassuming man of courage and faith you are. Especially over the past year, you amazed everyone around you with your quiet sense of peace and strength. You have touched many people and made a difference in many lives, and you have always been there to lend a helping hand to anyone.

We have traveled many places together to see the most beautiful sunrises and sunsets and we have exquisite memories of these. The sun has set on a portion of our lives, but since Monday when you physically left this earth, we have had the most glorious sunrises. In every one of them, I feel your presence, smiling and telling me, 'I'm alright. Everything is okay now.'

I admired your determination to fight this nasty disease. During the past year, we have witnessed many miracles together. God has been so good and we have been so blessed. We have had wealth in the form of our many friends and family members.

I look forward to the day we will be reunited for our eternal life together. In the meantime, enjoy paradise with all those who have passed into Life before you. You have earned your great reward. God loves you Larry, and so do I. Dianne."

Pastor Mike cleared his throat, wiped away a tear, and went on to say that Larry and I were quite a team. He ended by saying that Larry was surely in heaven shooting a 65 for 18 holes, and playing the big *The Price Is Right* game in the sky. It lightened up a very emotional moment. The vocalist beautifully sang, "The Wind Beneath My Wings," which was always one of Larry's favorite songs. *"Did you*

Dianne Klancir

ever know that you're my hero, and everything I wish I could be? I can fly higher than an eagle, for you are the wind beneath my wings." © Magnificent words—words I was sure I had never fully expressed to my husband.

As the service came to an end, we sang "How Great Thou Art," Larry's favorite hymn; one he could never sing completely through without welling up with tears. I did my best to sing it as loudly as I could in his honor, but I broke down and wept more than once.

The memorial service bulletin included a letter that Dina had written about her dad.

"To the family and friends of my father:

I want to start off by thanking you for being here today to celebrate my dad's life, for that IS what we are doing. My dad would not want anyone to mourn his passing, but instead to remember him as a loving husband and father, a loyal friend, and a hard worker. Our physical existence is only a blink of time on Earth. It is the spiritual existence that is passed on through the generations, and I feel my dad with me in spirit now like a guardian angel. His smile can be seen in the bright rays of the sun breaking through the clouds. As a child growing up with a father that was about 25 years older than most of my friends' fathers, I came to the realization fairly early in my life that his day of passing would probably come sooner than theirs. I truly believe that he knew this too, and through the life lessons and values he taught me, he prepared me for this event. The greatest gifts he gave me were those of strength, autonomy, and caring for others. He and my mom were perfect complements, and she is an amazing woman herself. I am blessed to be the child of this loving couple.

Thank you all again for the continuous prayers and assistance you have given my family in the past year. We are blessed to have all of you in our lives. My dad was a fighter, and battled his cancer until the end. Please keep his spirit alive and remember all the joyous times you had with him. He is an inspiration! Peace, Dina."

THE GIFT OF TODAY

Her letter was not something she was asked to write, but rather something she felt compelled to write. She touched many people with her words.

Following the service, we went to the fellowship hall to form a receiving line. I had never been hugged by so many well-wishers in my life. It felt like the steady flow of people would never end. Some of them had me laughing as they shared humorous stories about my Larry. Others had me in tears as they shared. Some were just speechless and hugged me for what seemed like an eternity without saying a word. I appreciated all of it. Looking at the posters of Larry's life, people were amazed at how gracefully he had aged. Following the luncheon, we returned to the house, and while many people visited together, I laid across my bed and rested. I was exhausted.

That night the house emptied of relatives returning to their homes, and only my parents and Dina and Adam remained. I slept through the night for the first time since Larry's passing. I felt a sense of peace come over me. It was done. I had done everything that Larry wanted me to, except for the disposal of his ashes. That would take time.

The following morning, my parents packed up to return home. It was a difficult goodbye for all of us. It gave Dina, Adam and I time to talk and visit together for the first time in a week. They seemed to be doing okay, and we talked about how pleased we knew Larry was with his service. On Monday, I asked Dina and Adam to return home. They didn't want to leave, but I couldn't ask them to continue to stay. I had to face the fact, sooner or later, that I was going to be living alone. Dina and I hugged each other endlessly and I practically pushed them out the door.

When the door closed behind them, I threw myself against it and wept for over an hour. It felt so strange to be in that big house all alone. There had been so many people crossing that threshold in the past several months, let alone days. I hadn't had a moment to myself to think or dream or feel in so long. Now that I had it, I didn't know if I wanted it. I kept looking around at the rooms as if I were walking

Dianne Klancir

in a strange house. Everything seemed different. It was so quiet, but when I actually sat down and just closed my eyes, there was a sense of comfort in it all. There was a peacefulness about it that embraced me and I felt Larry's presence around me everywhere.

Dina called several times that week to see how I was doing. I continued to stay home from work on Monday and Tuesday. I thought I would remain home the rest of the week, but by Wednesday morning I had had enough of being home alone, and returned to work. Those first few days back were difficult at best. I was happy to be there among my friends, but it was so hard to concentrate. The consumers were all so excited that I had finally returned after being gone almost two weeks. They had apparently been told by staff that my husband had passed away, and some of them were tearful as they hugged me. Deaths are always hard for the developmentally disabled to handle. Some of them grieve right away. Others don't feel the grief until months later. Larry was so kind to all of them, and they remembered him fondly.

When I got home in the evenings, I worked on memorials and thank-you notes. It took me a couple weeks to write them all because I wrote a special note in each one. We were blessed to be able to give memorial money to each of the four establishments chosen. The generosity and outpouring of love was overwhelming.

The following weekend was Dina's birthday. Adam had invited me to come into Aurora and join them for dinner to celebrate. He had picked up her engagement ring, and was planning to give it to her at the restaurant that evening and wanted me to be there. I felt like I was intruding on a very romantic, personal moment in their lives, but he insisted that he wanted me to be a part of that event. We went to Walter Payton's restaurant, which was like a museum dedicated to the famous Chicago Bear on one side and a restaurant on the other. (A difficult place for a Packer fan to be!) I gave Dina my gift at the apartment before we left for the restaurant and Adam carried along a little gift bag that he presented to her at the table when we were finally seated.

THE GIFT OF TODAY

He was on an absolute adrenalin rush that evening. Nothing could calm him down. He flitted around and nervously paced back and forth. He wanted everything to be perfect. The waiter sat us in a semi-circular booth and Adam presented Dina with the gift bag of bath and body items. Then he gave her a card to read that gave directions about putting the card down and looking straight ahead. When she did that, Adam was down on one knee in the middle of the restaurant, holding Dina's ring in his hand and asking her to marry him. It was the sweetest thing I had ever witnessed. He was totally oblivious to the fact that everyone else in the restaurant was staring at him. He only had eyes for Dina. She absolutely beamed and accepted his proposal. The waiter immediately brought champagne and the three of us toasted their engagement....again! I of course, was crying and wishing Larry had been there to share the moment with us. Then I realized something. Larry WAS there with us. I could feel his spirit all around us. We had a tantalizing meal and a very enjoyable evening.

That night I stayed at Dina and Adam's apartment on the living room sofa. I woke up the next morning with a whopping sinus headache. I could barely breathe. Dina asked if I would go to the Bridal Shoppe near their home "just to look." I laughed and agreed, although I would rather have had someone put me out of my misery. I had looked forward to this day all my life, shopping for my only daughter's wedding dress. It was the day that mothers dream of for years. But, my nose was all stuffed up, I had post-nasal drip, I couldn't breathe, I was running a low grade fever, coughing and my eyes were watering. Just what a mother wants on the day she has waited for all her life!

Naturally, Dina looked beautiful in each dress she tried on. We finally narrowed the search to two dresses. One was much showier and quite pricey; the other was simply elegant and just seemed to scream out Dina's name. She could not make up her mind and wanted so badly for me to decide. I could not make that decision for her and tried my best not to sway her either way. She finally picked the latter when a passerby stopped to stare at her and told her she was "absolutely stunning in that dress." I could not believe we were buying her wedding dress that day. Things were happening so fast. Dina agreed to let me take the dress home so that Adam would not see it before the wedding.

When we pulled up and he saw a large white zippered bag in the back seat, he looked at us in disbelief that she had found her gown already. We talked a little about the type of wedding the two of them envisioned. They wanted to keep things relatively simple. I told them I would do some checking into reception halls and availability of outdoor sites for a wedding ceremony. They didn't want to be married inside a church but rather outside in a garden by a minister.

Hours passed into days, and days into weeks. I was caught up in the throes of planning a wedding for my only daughter, by myself, and mourning the death of my husband. I truly believe that God gave me this pleasant distraction to help me make it through that difficult time in my life. Friends also called, invited me to dinner or stopped by, and it was so wonderful to know people were still thinking of me.

A couple weeks after Larry's memorial service, the funeral director appeared at my door. In his hand was a simple cardboard box about the size of a house brick. Inside the box were my husband's ashes. I looked at that box in amazement and realized for the first time that this is what Larry's life had been reduced to–a small box of ashes. The funeral director knew that we had plans to scatter the ashes somewhere, and therefore an urn was never discussed.

I called Dina that evening, in tears, to let her know I had the ashes. I brought them up to the bedroom, then down to the family room, then to his workroom, then back up to the bedroom. I didn't know what to do with them. Several days later, Dina and I decided to scatter them

THE GIFT OF TODAY

at the golf course on Father's day, which was Larry's wish in his last few months.

On Father's Day, June 16, 2002, Dina, Adam and I met our pastor at the golf course at 5:30 a.m. We walked to the 5th hole and stood at the tee-off box. Pastor Mike prayed as we bowed our heads. We each put on gloves and reached into the box and began sprinkling Larry's ashes from the tee all the way down the fairway until we reached the water. Then we continued on the other side of the water, down the fairway, to the green and into the hole. The morning dew was heavy on the grass, and the trail of ashes was visibly apparent all the way from the tee to the hole. We smiled with tears in our eyes as we gazed at it and knew that Larry would be pleased. He had finally made it over the water!

Happy Father's Day, Larry, and congratulations—it was a hole in one!

EPILOGUE

There were many times in my life that I didn't feel the presence of God, and I wondered if He heard me or cared about me. What I didn't acknowledge until a terminal diagnosis infiltrated our lives was that God was there all along. He was waiting for my heart to soften and be open enough to receive Him. I was a worrier. I wanted to be in charge of everything and thought nothing could possibly succeed in my life, unless I had the final word on it. Truth be told, I never had the final word on anything, but especially not my husband's destiny. Do I slip back into those old patterns? Sometimes. But I quickly try to bring myself back to reality by remembering I am not in control, nor do I need to be. I no longer need all the answers. I trust that God will provide them when He feels I need to know them.

Strange as it sounds, I know people who believe that death only happens to others and that they are going to live forever. We weren't meant to be here for very long. This is the practice field for the "big game". People have asked me if I am upset with God that he didn't heal my husband. What an interesting question! My husband was healed in a much better place than this. It was his time to leave his earthly life. For people who haven't dealt with their own mortality, this is a difficult concept. Do I miss my husband? Of course. There isn't a day that I don't think about him. Am I angry at God? Absolutely not. To be angry at God would mean not understanding that death is an important part of life.

THE GIFT OF TODAY

My daughter Dina was married on May 17, 2003 in a beautiful garden in Ashton, Illinois. The weather was perfect, and my daughter looked beautiful. She walked down a long flight of stairs through the three-tiered garden towards her guests, and as she descended the steps, the sun shone so brightly it hurt our eyes. Larry was not there physically, but his spirit was felt by everyone at that ceremony.

Larry's oldest son is a cancer survivor, and has had to take a disability retirement. It is my understanding that his cancer was a direct result of Agent Orange he was exposed to during his tour of duty in Vietnam. He spends his days babysitting for his granddaughter.

There are days my life is more difficult than others. There are times I feel very lonely and ache for my husband. But I have learned to walk through the pain and turn to God for strength. I have great memories of a terrific man – not a perfect man – but one that loved me until the day he died.

If God's presence isn't felt in your life, may I suggest some quiet time talking one-on-one with Him. When I learned to speak to God from my heart and listen for the response, I was never without an answer. This type of communication with God allows me to soul search, define who I am, and the plans God has for me. But, we have to be open to hear the message.

We are all unique individuals, with our own special talents and gifts. I didn't want my entire life to pass me by without recognizing what my purpose was here, and God has pointed me in the direction to discover those gifts. Enjoy every day – you never know when it will be your last one. Laugh, live and treasure every moment.

"Yesterday is history, Tomorrow is a mystery. And today? Today is a gift. That's why it's called the present." (by Babatunde Olatunji).

ISBN 142510949-7